D1195821

HEARTBREAK - PROOF

Beyond Bubble Baths and Wine to True Self-Love

Hali Winch

Heartbreak-proof: Beyond bubble baths and wine to true self-love

ISBN: 978-1-7365114-0-4

www.hailswinch.com

For my past. Thank you for getting me to where I am now. I would not be the Hails writing this book without you.

Table of Contents

"We waste a lot of time building an image we want the world to see instead of taking responsibility for breaking through the limits we create in our own heads and becoming who we were made to be."

— Jordan Lee Dooley, **Own Your Everyday: Overcome the Pressure to Prove and Show Up for What You're Made to Do**

CHAPTER 1
Who is this Quack?

You're right, I probably should introduce myself prior to writing an entire book on this concept of "love." So hi, I'm Hali Winch. There are probably very few of you who even know me, and if you do know me—thanks for actually purchasing my book, friends! Anywho, the question of who I am is a very complex one, I can promise you that. As you'll learn throughout the entirety of this book, I am more than just one role, as are you.

Let me begin by telling you a few of the hats that I wear. One of my most well-known roles that I play is the middle child, the only girl, and the go-getting, overachieving daughter who belongs to the Winch Family. Those who know me know that I have two brothers, one older who goes by Cori, and one younger who we call Bailey; just about anyone who comes into contact with them fawn over them. They're great and all, but they are part of the reason why I'm writing this book (love you guys!). Then there are my amazingly loving parents, Tess and John, who adore me with eyes larger than the world; they're seriously the best. But, as with any author, they are part of the reason that I am writing this book as well.

Aside from being an awesome daughter and kick-ass sister (most days), I'm also a fifth-grade special education teacher. This is one of my most noble hats that I wear. I have wanted to be a teacher for as long as I remember. The most rewarding day that I ever had was the day that I finally received my New York State teacher certification. Teaching is one of my greatest passions, and honestly a cornerstone for the purpose of this book. So before I get too far along, a huge shout-out to all of my kiddos I have had over the years—you guys have inspired me to channel my ADD and craziness into writing a book that (hopefully) inspires others to look at love in a much more multidimensional manner.

Finally, and most curiosity sparking, I wear the hat of an intuitive medium. Now, I know what you are probably thinking—*she really is a quack*. But, hear me out. We are all intuitive to a certain degree. This is what you will learn throughout this book and on the track to love, specifically self-love. I have been an intuitive medium for my entire life. However, I only started practicing when I was twenty years old. Being an intuitive medium has changed my life entirely. It has caused me to look at people, situations, and especially aspects of life, such as love, in a different light. I will dive into this a little bit more later on in this book, but the important takeaway here is: I'm not as different from you as you may think.

I can imagine you're probably wondering why the heck all of these hats had to be explained to you. Trust me, the last thing I enjoy doing is talking in detail about myself, and especially my emotions. However, my hats I wear and the roles I play and the emotions I've experienced impact the overall message of this book, and ultimately led me to where I am today.

If you were to just look at the cover of this book, or to even see my Instagram, you would probably think that I was just a regular old Upstate New York gal looking to get a vodka cran from a bar in downtown Saratoga on a beautiful summer night. And honestly, you're not completely wrong. You see, I am just a normal girl who kills for a good vodka cran and a night filled with music and dancing, but I, as well as you, are so much more than just one hat that we wear.

That leads me to my next, and biggest point of this entire book: **We are more than the expectations set for us that indicate the love we think we deserve.**

Whoa, loaded statement. I don't expect you to know exactly what I mean based on that one sentence, but maybe you do! If you do, PROUD OF YOU, because it took me twenty-four years to get here. If you don't, then SAME, because I'm still figuring it out as I write this book. My point being, we are living in a world that sets parameters or expectations for us. Based on these expectations, such as posts on social media, external influences, relationships we are involved in, etc., we begin to develop an idea of the love we think we want or even deserve.

Think about it: how many of you reading this book see posts on TikTok, Snapchat, Instagram, Facebook, Twitter and think, *What am I doing that I don't deserve this type of love?* Well, consider me your knight-in-shining-armor, because I'm here to tell you that this type of "love" has nothing to do with what you are doing, but rather what you are not doing for yourself. You see, we're raised to believe that "love" is an external feeling we get from others, which is so far from the truth that it's laughable.

It took me five-ever to figure out what exactly I was doing (or rather, not doing) to attract the type of love that I deserve. Wanna know the real kicker? It all had to do with the love I was giving myself. You see, we are taught from the earliest years of our lives that we experience love externally; that is, we experience love as an emotion with other people we surround ourselves with in our lives.

If we are lucky enough to grow up in a household that has two loving parents, that is our first experience of love. If not, we may begin our understanding of love through a single parent, grandparent, sibling, aunt, or a caretaker. Perhaps your family was involved in church, and you learn that love is formed between you and God, or Adam and Eve. Either way, we learn from the earliest of times that love is something that is formed between two people or beings. What a load of crap!

There is quite a big difference in the love we find in others, and the love we have for ourselves. You see, this notion we call love that we seem to receive from the earliest of times is perpetuated onto us from others, but that's not where the feeling of love comes from. We do not feel loved because those around us love us. Instead, we feel love inside of us because that belongs to us. We are filled with love ourselves. And once we hone in on this love, we begin to love others that same way. It's a reciprocal process, but it begins first and foremost within us. After mastering the art of love with ourselves, then comes the Adam and Eve and mushy gushy love stuff.

Personally, I grew up with two parents who had (and still do have) a pocket full of love for my brothers and me. I was also extremely fortunate to have brothers, aunts, uncles, cousins, grandparents, neighbors … you get the point. All of those people in my direct micro system and mesosystem (thanks, six years of education classes) made up my conceptual understanding of what love is. This includes all of those lovely people who I've had the privilege of knowing in my life. Lucky for me, most of these people in my life gave me genuine love. I also was lucky in that mostly all of those in my life were involved in relationships that were genuine. So I bet you're wondering why in the world I'm complaining about love and standing on my soapbox and preaching to you all about love? Well, because there is so much more to love than the external relationships we grow up seeing.

Remember my statement before? All of these relationships we grow up with set expectations for the love that we think we deserve. Now, I'm not saying it's my parents' fault for loving me the way they did and causing me to have the expectation for a man to love me the way I deserve. What I am saying is that just because I have the expectation for someone to love me a certain way, doesn't mean it will just happen. In fact, very rarely does it actually happen.

Now, I'm not saying that amazing love stories don't happen every single day. Absolutely not. In fact, people I consider my best friends are involved in Nicholas Sparks-type love stories that leave me with the warm and fuzzies. But there's a catch—those involved in these amazing love stories didn't hold the expectation of finding unconditional love with someone else. Yup, you heard me. Instead, they found that love within themselves, and had it mirrored back at them by someone else. There's the difference.

The same holds true for those of you reading this who didn't have the opportunity to experience unconditional love from a young age. The good news is, none of us are doomed. As you'll learn throughout the book, I am far from a doom-and-gloom type of person. I think this may come from the fact that I'm a teacher and intuitive medium, or the fact that I'm just a sucker for a good romcom. Either way, I wouldn't set out to write this book if it was going to lead you to failure.

Instead, I am going to lead you on the most soul-quenching, breathtaking, self-indulgent experience of a lifetime. I bet that piqued your curiosity a bit, but I also bet you're not quite sold. After all, I am just a twenty-four-year-old woman who has never been married nor found a husband—no doubt he's out there, though, or perhaps he's reading this himself. And you're also right if you're thinking I'm just a teacher in a small town who practices her intuitive mediumship with whatever clients are thrown her way. You are absolutely not wrong in your accusations. But I will bust your chops for a quick second—

Yes, I am a twenty-four-year-old single woman living in her parents' basement apartment while teaching and maintaining a healthy group of clients; thank you for noticing! However, I am much more than these labels. I am much more than the expectations that have been put forth for me my entire life. And I bet you guessed it: I have learned to grow beyond the expectations of love that have been given for me to live by. I am by no means the guru of love. But, I can share my personal experience of what it is like to break these labels of love, break the expectations of love, and rejoice in the fact that love is so much more than a term used to describe an emotion between two people.

Love lives within each of us every day. Most of us don't know how to evoke such a feeling within ourselves enough to give it to others and therefore have it mirrored back to us. Or maybe you love others too much, so much that you don't know how to love yourself. That's why I'm writing this. I know a bit about not loving myself, which in turn has caused turmoil in my life, in my relationships, and in my mental health.

The purpose of this book is to cause a young girl going through a tumultuous relationship to stop and think about how she can emulate this love within her. The purpose of this book is to make the mother of three stop for ten minutes each day and read a chapter in this book and realize she is doing everything so friggin' right, except she's not saving enough love for herself. Maybe the purpose of this book is for the basketball, lax, and football jocks to stop for a second and think how they can fulfill themselves with love rather than look for an empty hookup to satisfy them for the night.

Whatever resonates with you, I will try to make that connection. The biggest takeaway I want you to have is how to make yourself heartbreak-proof by loving yourself enough. My point is, this book is far beyond scratching the surface of finding love. No, it's a book that will teach you how to fill yourself with love, so much so that you can attract it with no bounds, unconditionally. In order to do that, you will have to buckle up, grab some ice cream, silence your iPhone and SmartTV and enjoy the messy (but worth it) ride to a town I like to call Self-Love.

CHAPTER 2
What the Hell is Self-Love?

If you are anything like me, this term "self-love" has been thrown around a lot in your life. *You need to invest in some self-love. Once you love yourself everything will be different.* And of course: *Clearly she doesn't love herself by the way she acts.* I'm sure we have heard it all at this point. People are so quick to throw the word out there, but they have the darndest time just putting words or characteristics to such a vague term in order to define it. What in the nutcracker does "self-love" even mean? Or better yet, what does it even look like? And most importantly, how is self-love going to make me heartbreak-proof, as Morgan Wallen sang in "Whiskey Glasses"? Well, well, let me help you with all of these burning questions.

I can remember one of the first times I ever heard this term. I was a sophomore in high school, and I had the biggest crush on a senior at our school. I can remember each day daydreaming as I walked down the senior hallway that this boy, we'll call him Will, would sweep me off my feet and whisk me away for a magical, romantic relationship. Will was my first real crush. He and I had flirted the entire winter months together, making eyes at one another from across the lunchroom, and me cheering excessively for him at basketball games. Whenever we would hang around each other, we were constantly flirting. Well, a couple months and several flirty texts later, we finally became an "item." Let me tell you, our "itemness" was the furthest thing from what I expected going into high school.

Growing up, I was obsessed with good romantic stories. Nicholas Sparks' novels, Troy Bolton and Gabriella Montez, Taylor Swift and her next-door neighbor in her "You Belong With Me" music video. I was quite the dreamer. I went into high school with the expectation that I was going to fall madly in love with this jock who typically wouldn't notice me. He would gaze at me from afar, we would lock eyes, and the rest would be absolute history!

Boy, was I wrong when I met Will. First of all, we met through my oldest brother because they were best friends. Second of all, we live in a culture that is technology obsessed and feels that the most sensible form of communication should happen through a mini computer we keep in our back pockets (not hating on technology, but you see what I'm saying). So, going into this "relationship" with Will, I expected him to play the role of a boyfriend.

Well, I guess we both had a different point of view on what a relationship consisted of. We flirted, hooked up, cuddled, and then ghosted one another. When we were at school, I noticed that he wouldn't look in my direction anymore. Even worse, he pretended as if we had never met before—can you say *rude*? Okay, okay, no biggie. I would tell myself it was because he didn't want others to know of his love for me. Duh, obviously! That must be it! Cue what I like to call—the hookup dates. That is simply what it was for Will and me. We would meet up on his terms, hook up, then pretend as if we didn't know each other until he wanted to hook up again. At the ripe age of fifteen, I thought that this was what a relationship and love was. I thought begging for someone's attention and meeting them on their terms was what it meant to be dating someone and falling in love with one another. I mean, it was working to some extent, because we were hanging out regularly, we were just doing so while shoving our tongues down each other's throats!

I'm sure you have already guessed it, but May came around and Will ghosted me one final time. I would text him, try to flirt with him, and stare him up and down in hopes that he would make eye contact with me in the lunchroom. Sadly, it was as if I wasn't even there anymore. No texts back, no conversations in any form, and definitely no stolen looks over our burnt grilled cheeses, either.

I was sooo confused. I remember asking my friends if a break-up had to be a mutual agreement, or if one person can just leave you without saying a word. Of course to these questions they all looked at me like I had five heads. After about 174 text messages and one final meet-up, I learned, much to my surprise, that Will and I had not been dating in the slightest bit. Instead, he informed me that I was just easy and a fun girl to pass some time with. I'm sorry ... what did you say, Will?

Talk about devastation. Oh my. I did not think there were enough tears in my body to cry as much as I did over Will. Thank god Taylor Swift released her song "15" to get me through my worst "breakup" I thought I would ever experience! (Stay tuned for chapter thirteen about Dave.) I cried for a whole month; I even wallowed in self-pity. Finally, my best friends had had enough of my bitching and moaning over Will. They decided to confront me with a hard truth—you need to have more respect for yourself.

I was utterly confused and quite frankly off the deep end that my best friends were failing to see the heartbreak I had just been put through. Was it not obvious that Will and I had been dating and in love for the past six months? It may not have been clear to them that we were dating, but what was clear was the lack of love I had for myself—hence the comment about respect (ouch!).

I can remember my best friend telling me as we piled into her 1997 Toyota 4Runner, *Hails, once you learn to love yourself, the right boy will come right to you.* I stopped dead in my tracks when those words came out of her mouth. Love myself? Don't I already love myself? How could she say such a thing? Darn her! Shut up and drive me to McDonald's, so I can continue to cry about Will and shove my mouth full of french fries and a chocolate shake! How about that for loving myself! That was over ten years ago, and I remember her exact sentence and the reaction I had to her words. I percolated over that remark for years. I never really understood what she even meant by that. After all, if I didn't love myself, what had I been doing for all of these years? Was it really that important that I loved who I was in order to find someone to love me? Well, apparently my fifteen-, sixteen-, seventeen-, eighteen- (and many more versions) year-old self did not feel that was true.

Despite not believing in what she said, I was still curious as to what loving myself or "self-love" even meant. I would ask myself every night before I went to bed, *What does that look like? How can I quickly do that so my Prince Charming will come sweep me off my feet? How will I ever love myself with how I look?* I would dwell on the feeling of love and how fast I could convince myself that I did love myself, despite being overweight, unattractive, short, too broad for a girl, and so many other labels that I put on myself. I spent hours Googling the definition, and to this day, this is the best definition I could scrounge up for it.

Let's look at self-love for a second. The dictionary definition of it is:

self-love[self-luhv] *noun:*
1. the instinct by which one's actions are directed to the promotion of one's own welfare or well-being, especially an excessive regard for one's own advantage.[1]

If you're anything like me, dictionary definitions do nothing for you. So, let's break this down, shall we?

Self-love, by nature, is the act of doing something for yourself that benefits you and only you directly. This type of love is deemed "selfish" more often than not because instead of benefiting all of those around us (I know you are one of those bleeding hearts, too), we do things that are going to benefit ourselves. When I first started researching this topic, I began looking for information on Pinterest on how to engage in "self-love activities." Oftentimes we look to social media to tell us how to do it, which defeats the purpose of doing it. I can't tell you how many times I've been on Twitter or Facebook and have seen a picture of a girl sitting in the tub eating a box of chocolate with a glass of wine and the meme is labeled "self-

---

1 "Self-Love." *Dictionary.com.*

love." Yes, that is one form of it, but the form of self-love targeted in this book goes far beyond the surface of doing nice things for yourself. Furthermore, the type of self-love I want you to achieve is the one that will mend the broken hearts, and make you heart-break-proof for the future.

For example, when I first heard of this term way back when Will was fooling around with me, I thought this simple yet loaded term simply meant doing what I want, when I want. So for my fifteen-year-old self, that looked a lot like eating fried food, taking some bubble baths here and there, and gossiping with friends. This is the stuff that I thought made me feel "good" about myself. After all, I did enjoy the grease-loaded fries and the lavender scent I would walk away with! But boy was I soooo wrong. You see, for so long we think of self-love as things that help us feel good in the moment. What about after that moment passes? After the five minutes it takes you to devour a large fry or the hour-long bath you sank yourself into? Do you love yourself then? Do you feel empowered to make a better life for yourself? If you're being honest with yourself, the answer is probably no.

I learned with time that these minuscule activities and tangibles were merely tiding me over until my next batch of self-loathing occurred. They were a Band-Aid over a bullet hole. And for those of you who are women reading this, you know what a fifteen-year-old, or shoot, even a fifty-three-year-old can dwell on, loathing for hours. Since I just burst your bubble about what we think self-love is based on, like the societal norms that are created for us on social media (i.e., a girl sitting in a bathtub eating cake and holding a glass of wine—come on, we've all seen that meme), I am here to give you a much deeper understanding of self-love.

Before you shut this book and refuse to reopen it again, also know that some forms of self-love can take place in a bubble bath or a large fry from McDonald's (nothing compares sometimes!). But, the purpose of self-love is to be able to love yourself more than those around you could. Self-love enables you to be by yourself for a while, and to be completely comfortable with that. It is the act of feeling good about yourself, even on the days when you feel bloated, cheated on your diet, or did some other unspeakable things you may not be so proud about. It's digging deeper within yourself to help heal your wounds, heal your soul, and finding what lights you up in order to love yourself and your life. It's the ability to have someone walk away from you, and not be heartbroken. It's becoming heartbreak-proof altogether.

So, yes, those teeny-tiny tasks that have been mentioned above may make you feel good in the moment of your self-loathing, but the goal is to not have to get to self-loathing. My goal is to get you to the point where you no longer hate yourself so much that you turn to food or mindless activities to make yourself feel better. After all, we want to enjoy our lives, and self-love is just the key to doing so!

One of the most prominent keys to self-love is being able to make changes. Clearly, there are obstacles that are standing in your way and preventing you from loving yourself the way you deserve to! So, take a second to think about them. What do you feel are the biggest "things" about yourself that are preventing you from looking in the mirror and saying *OOOOOOOO GIRL! You're killing it, look at you go!* every time you see yourself? The goal is to feel like Lizzo as she sings "Good As Hell" when we are with ourselves!

Here is a challenge—make a list of *everything* that you feel is a barrier to your self-love. Believe it or not, making a list will help you to not only visualize all of your barriers in written form, but it will also help you to decipher what is standing in your way. Once your list of obstacles is created, try to brainstorm one way you can change each obstacle. Granted, some situations are out of our hands, and I will touch on that in a second. But for now, try to create as many solutions to your obstacles as possible! Ready, set, go!

***

Okay, have your list? If not, be sure to do it at some point today or tonight. I promise you, it's going to be the first stepping stone on your path to divine love within yourself! Now, hitting on the point of the list—change. We as humans get so settled into our habits of life. I mean, who likes to change things up, anyway? I'll tell you who—me! The problem with habits is, sometimes they do not always benefit us the best way they should. Remember, self-love is when we choose actions, things, or people that benefit *us*!

Here is an example: Growing up, I have always loved food. I remember being six years old and telling myself that I couldn't wait to be older, so I can eat whatever I want, whenever I want, without an adult telling me what to eat or how much to eat. I mean come on, who wouldn't love ice cream for breakfast? Well, as the years progressed, I began to have an unhealthy relationship with food, because of this desperate need to control what I ate and how much I ate. When I went to my four-year college, I felt like I was finally able to eat the way I wanted to. As a result, I ate about five meals a day, most of which were fried or processed in some way. I gained thirty pounds within two years, and was the most miserable I had ever been. I would wake up, look in the mirror, and cry at the image that was reflected back to me (so *not* a Lizzo moment).

When I would eat, I would tell myself it was okay, because I was choosing foods that I wanted rather than ones that were actually good for my body. Whenever I was sad, I would choose chocolate. Whenever I was out, I would choose fried foods because I didn't know how to make them myself. I chose to celebrate life by going out to eat with friends. I would tell myself I was indulging in self-love because I wasn't being hard on myself, or making myself throw up like other girls did, just because I ate something bad. However, the horrifying image I would see every morning was nothing short of a slap in the face, starting an endless spiral of loathing for allowing myself to eat the way I did the day before. Before long, I was weighing in at 205 pounds. I remember the day that I saw that number on the scale, and I cried harder than I ever had in my life. It was right around the time I had hit absolute rock bottom in my life. That was when I chose to begin this journey that I am now taking you on as well: finding out how to truly love who I am.

My habit of binge-eating unhealthy food was what I identified as the top obstacle I faced that prohibited my ability to love my-self. I put a star on that one, underlined it, and created a solution—learn healthy eating habits that I can sustain for the entirety of my life. Cue the light show paired with angels singing! If only that was what it was like. No, instead the choice to change my eating habits was hard. However, I was dedicated to making my life better, and to not having the feeling of guilt, disgust, or utter horror flood my mind anymore when I looked in the mirror. I started out by down-loading the Noom[2] app, and over the course of a few months I was able to tackle my biggest barrier that stood in the way of me loving who I was (on the outside, that is).

Coinciding with my unhealthy food relationship, I also had ad-opted personality traits and characteristics from others over the years. Let me tell you, they were not cute either. Not by a landslide. Instead of taking on traits such as caring and kindness, and char-acteristics like good flirting techniques and controlled social cues, I instead inherited things like an odd accent in my voice that made absolutely no sense at all, a laugh so loud it could wake up folks in Texas, and the ability to twist a tale better than the boy who cried wolf. The worst part? For the longest time I thought these traits were helping me attract people into my life that would stay. Instead they just drove them away without me consciously realizing it!

Now, I know we all have various obstacles that we all face. Maybe you don't have the best family in your life, and one of your biggest obstacles is that they are constantly negative. Negativity

---

2 *Noom.* Noom, Inc., 2019. https://web.noom.com/terms-and-conditions-of-use/

is one of the most influential things that can create an obstacle to how we love ourselves. This is one that may not be as easy to create a solution for, or unfortunately, it may cause some uncomfortable changes. For example, maybe your sister is a Negative Nancy who is constantly making you feel poorly about your decisions. Or maybe, it is your father who makes you feel insecure. A possible solution for long-term self-love would be setting a boundary with them. Let that person know exactly how they are making you feel! After all, they feel it necessary for you to know their opinion; make it known that you have one as well! Unfortunately, we as humans also succumb to other people's opinions and judgements of ourselves. In this instance, for this obstacle, cutting a toxic person out may be just the kind of self-love that you need.

Again, these changes are ones that are going to create lifelong effects. I'm not saying to create solutions that may make today, tomorrow, or the next day easier. In fact, I'm saying quite the opposite. Changes that are worth making are often the hardest ones that we endure. Giving up all of my comfort food I ate while growing up was the equivalent of a person leaving my life. Food had always been my comfort, and when I finally made the choice to let it go, I was liberated. The same holds true for the obstacle that you are facing yourself. Once we can choose to change that obstacle, and let it go, we begin down a road of benefiting ourselves for the best! And I can attest, that benefit is one that continues for a lifetime (take my word for it).

So, here is your first stepping stone for this journey. Take some time and make that list. Write down every little thing that you feel is standing in your way of loving yourself wholeheartedly, authentically. Make the list in order, starting with the one obstacle you feel is the biggest. For me, it was my physical appearance and personality traits I had acquired. For you, it may be someone in your life, something that happened in your past that you can't seem to forgive yourself for, or any number of obstacles that feel right for YOU.

Once you have them written down, think of those scary changes. Think of the ways that you can overcome those obstacles for life-time success! Maybe it's therapy, moving away, or committing to an exercise regimen. The best part is, you get to choose how you want to change to resolve your obstacle!

Lastly, and most importantly, I need you to commit to working toward overcoming one of your obstacles. It may not be your biggest one. Maybe you need to start with the most minor one on your list. It doesn't matter, because this is your journey! Pick one of those obstacles, and commit today to start the motion of change. Call that counselor up! Delete their number from your phone! Start that mile jog! Whatever it is, make the conscious choice to do it now. Trust me, you'll thank me later!

Now to answer your burning question from the start of this chapter—self-love is the key to becoming heartbreak-proof. Re-read that last sentence. In order to become heartbreak-proof, you have to love yourself enough to set up boundaries for yourself, and respect yourself enough to not let someone else take control over your choices, opinions, or actions. We'll dive into this more in the rock-bottom chapter, but at least you have the short on how to become heartbreak-proof!

CHAPTER 3

First Comes Love, Then Comes ...?

O kay, now that we have some idea of what self-love is versus what it can easily be mistaken as, let's talk about the other kind of love. Ya know, the kind that we are all pretty much striving for in our lives, and more likely than not, ends up leaving us heartbroken? Ah, yes. That mushy, gushy, Nicholas Sparks' romance that makes our hearts swell and worlds come to a shattering halt. If you are anything like me, you have waited your whole life for this unconditional love with someone who just "gets you." If not, maybe you have just waited for someone who merely tolerates you. Either way you slice it, we are all looking for someone to spend our lives with. After all, being that crazy cat lady or the rickety old man is not something any of us strive for. In fact, from an early age we're mostly taught that relationships, cohabitating, and of course, love are the purpose of living.

But how can we attract such love if we don't have the foundational piece that this whole book is based on? I spent my entire life searching high and low for this kind of love, but I would turn up with nothing but a broken heart and tear-stained cheeks. Lucky for you, I am going to go all intuitive-medium Hails on ya, and I'll let you in on a little secret when it comes to finding this "love" we strive for. You ready for it? Are you sure? Okay, it may be a bit of a letdown, but ...

You attract what you put out in the universe.

Ha ... ha ... ha ... what? *So this quack is saying that if I put out that I love myself the way I want, that love will come back to me? Like a boomerang?*

Well, yes. That is exactly what I'm saying. So let me break this down for you, because for me, this was one of the most bizarre concepts to grasp.

Remember Will? Let me give you the backstory on him real quick ...

I moved to a new school when I was in tenth grade. At my former school, I faced several issues with friends, teachers, community, boys—you name it. I was getting bullied by people I considered closest in my circle, my family faced turmoil for allowing my older brother to transfer schools, and of course as an awkward fourteen-year-old girl, I hadn't quite mastered the language of boy, either. Needless to say, my freshman year of high school was anything but glamorous. As a result, I became what the school (and I mean both peers and adults) referred to as a "mean girl." I would gossip, lie, and intentionally hurt others' feelings in hopes that it would make others love me. The worst part? I thought my actions would gain attention from the boys I had crushes on to get the girls who bullied me to like me. Needless to say, I was just labeled "the mean girl" and fell further and further down the coolness scale (and rightfully so!).

I was excited for my new school and a chance to meet new people so I could start off on the right foot. However, I found that at my new school, there were more people I wanted to impress, and I was continuously living in shoes I couldn't fill. I wanted to come off as cool, chill, pretty, athletic, popular, and many other labels that I didn't realize were not necessary. As I was striving to achieve all of these labels, I was reminded each day when I looked in the mirror that I hated myself, and I couldn't wait for a guy to just want to be my boyfriend. I would fall asleep thinking, *If a guy could just like me enough to kiss me and want to sleep with me, people would like me, too.*

Well, young grasshopper, ask and you shall receive. Only back then, I did not know of this golden rule that now facilitates my life. Whatever we speak into the universe, we get! In my case, I was breaking my own heart by refusing to love what I had, and as a result, I attracted a heart-breaker.

Given time and the chase of love, Will and I ended up becoming an item. Will was the quintessential jock. He was tall, athletic, funny, attractive, cool, popular. Ya know, he was all of those labels that I was trying to fulfill within myself. Amazing what I attracted! Anywho, as you read about in chapter two, the fling with Will was short-lived and burnt out quicker than it lit up my world. He was superficial, only wanted sex, and really was a pseudo-boyfriend who gave me exactly what I wanted in the first place—physical affection. Being only fifteen years old, I didn't know any better. I thought the world was out to get me. After all, how could the universe be so cruel? How could the universe be so unfair? Did it not see all of the love that I had in my heart for a boyfriend? Ugh! Well, looking back on it nine years later, the universe gave me exactly what I had asked it for and mirrored back the love I was putting out—heartbreaking.

Don't believe me yet? Let me give you another example from Hali's book of dating history. About six months after Will and I ended, I once again began speaking to the universe about what I longed for. I would tell my friends, "I want someone who is funny." I wanted a boy who was fun, would push the limits, but would also love me and think I was funny. At this point in time, I was aiming for the funny label, so my guy had to match my crazy. I would intentionally draw attention to myself so I could make jokes, cause others to laugh, or really do anything that would bring a smile to people's faces. I was stepping more into who I was, but I still struggled with who I actually was; ya know, beyond the labels and stuff. I would still continue to get people to like me by whatever means that took. Sure enough, what I was putting out into the universe, I was attracting in a relationship. Cue my first real-life relationship with my first real-life boyfriend. We'll call him Jerry.

Jerry was the school's clown and bad boy. At the point in time that I entered his life, he was known around school for getting suspended due to ripping donuts in his car on the school's softball field and getting a bird taped to the side of his head for shits and giggles when he was drunk. Did I tell you I wanted someone to match my crazy? Aside from these memorable stories, Jerry was a boy who could make just about anyone laugh. I really hadn't had much interaction with him throughout my time at Greenwich, aside from being in love with his best friend (that's Dave ... he'll come in later, I promise). Jerry was someone I had never really put much thought toward, but the night he came into my life was the night I felt everything all at once. Picture the Disney fireworks show going off while the song "Born to be Wild" blares in the background. I feel that was pretty symbolic of our relationship.

Despite his wild streak and the countless number of stories I could tell that occurred in our four-year-long relationship, Jerry was a guy who came into my life for a reason. We dated throughout my junior and senior years of high school, as well as my freshman and sophomore years of college. Not only was he able to make me laugh, but he was continuously challenging me to push my limits, try new things, and really be adventurous. He introduced me to people who became lifelong friends, who I didn't know would stay in my life as long as they did. When I was with Jerry, I felt as though I met someone who appreciated humor, while also thinking I hung the stars at night. However, as with all good things, it came to an end.

Eventually, Jerry's humor became less entertaining. I began falling out of love with the guy who refused to complete schoolwork, made inappropriate jokes, and enjoyed drinking just a little too much. I can remember the nights we would lay in bed, confessing our love to one another, thinking we were going to make it through to the end, just to hear my own heart remind me to pump the breaks just a little. Unfortunately, sophomore year of college, I learned that Jerry was falling out of love with me as well. I turned a blind eye to it for quite a few months, up until he met another, younger, funnier girl.

I was devastated, and yet again at square one. For the first month of our breakup, I seemed to be holding up okay. I hated Jerry, I hated his friend Dave, and I hated what I had been through. But, I kept reminding myself that it wasn't meant to be. I had once again attracted the wrong kind of love. Then, self-hatred settled in. I began looking in the mirror and saying things like, *He left you because you've gotten fat,* or *Dave probably told him about the way you feel about him, that he doesn't put in enough effort. Curse you for putting your heart on the line!*

The self-demoting comments never seemed to stop. For about three months, I would continuously hound my mind to the point where I couldn't do anything enjoyable without reminding myself how lousy I really was. The worst part of the breakup? Jerry had left me for another girl, and instead of realizing it was him not giving enough, I chose to think it was me not *being* enough. This is how social media and society has trained people to think—you get dumped, it's your fault. Someone doesn't like you? It's your fault. You didn't get that job promotion, but Susie from the office did? Yup, your fault! We grow up in a society that is extremely focused on our shortcomings and our failures, and as a result, we internalize those failures as not being enough for someone or something. We become heartbroken, and the worst part is, we are set up for this heartbreak throughout our lives. Why? Because we aren't taught that real love and appreciation comes from within, not from outside.

Think about the last failure you've had. It could be anything, epic or not. How much blame did you put on yourself? Did you say things to yourself like, *You're such an idiot, If only you tried harder,* or *You deserve to fail?* If you're anything like me, you probably had a mantra of this going through your head. We are so quick to judge ourselves when we fail. We are so used to the heartbreak that we easily assume it's our fault. You want to know why? We want to be the first person disappointed in ourselves before someone else has the chance to be. The funny thing is, this is the exact opposite of what actually happens.

Now again, I know what you're thinking! (Hello, intuitive medium, remember?) You're probably reading this and saying *No, you quack! When I fail, I recognize my failure and am hard on myself because I do deserve it! And everyone else in my life normally agrees with me!* We've all been there. Famous example from my life—I wanted to lose weight. I tried diet after diet for years, but just couldn't seem to lose the weight. I failed more times than I succeeded. Each time I failed, I would say to my mom, *Jeeze, I'm just going to be fat forever. I am so fat,* to which she would respond, *Oh I understand, I am much fatter than you.* Before I knew it, it turned into a fat-shaming contest with each other of who was fatter. I would acknowledge my failure at losing weight before she could, so I could spare myself her silent judgments or thoughts that I had yet to lose weight despite my efforts at another diet.

This whole scenario links directly with what this chapter is all about—you attract what you put out in the universe. Although I was not losing weight with whichever fad diet I had tried that week, putting myself down based on my failures was only attracting more failure. The comments I was making about myself attracted more negativity, or fat shaming, between my mother and me in order to deflect judgement. The more I negatively spoke to and of myself or with my mother about my shortcomings with weight loss, the more I was attracting the thought that it was indeed impossible to lose weight.

Want to know the craziest part of this whole process? Once I stopped the negative thoughts in regard to my failures with weight loss, you'll never guess what happened. Yup, I began actually losing weight! Each time I didn't lose weight, I began replacing my thoughts and comments to myself with *Eh, you tried hard. The weight will come off tomorrow.* Or, *Maybe try a different recipe to-*

night that you feel is healthier. I then began to speak these thoughts aloud to my mother. I would say things like, *I am excited to try this new recipe that I think will make my body feel good*, or, *I am really giving this all that I can in order to become healthier.* I even started to write in my journal *I am healthy. I am losing weight.* Well sure as sugar, about two months after I started doing that, I lost fourteen pounds! Score!

The same thing is true for my breakup with Jerry. Although I hounded myself for not being enough for him, I never once stopped to think about the lessons I learned from Jerry—and boy, was there a lot of them. With each negative comment about myself, I attracted more and more negativity. Ever heard the phrase, *When it rains, it pours?* Yeah, that was my dating life for about three years post-Jerry. As life continued and seasons changed, I grew a little and became more cognizant of the person I wanted to become. With this came more labels I threw on myself. I labeled myself as funny, intelligent, perfect, athletic, kind, outgoing, cheerleader, hard worker, etc. There were so many labels that my head began to spin. With each label I put on myself, I found that I was working overtime to not only live up to those labels, but also to look for them in guys. I wanted the smartest, most athletic and funny boy I could find on campus just so I felt more complete with myself. As we know, we attract what we put out in the universe. I won't share all of the lovely stories just yet, because I do have an entire book of lessons that comes with each. However, there is a very important message that is embedded in this chapter:

In order to attract the love we truly want and deserve, we have to find that love within ourselves. That means, ditching the labels and finding it within ourselves. It means becoming heartbreak-proof so a Will or Jerry or Dave doesn't fudge up your life like they did mine. I know, easier said than done. You see, we spend a majority of our lives trying to live up to labels or expectations that others put on us. Whether it is to be funny, smart, badass, or whatever—we are constantly trying to pursue a life we think other people will find attractive in us. The real knee-slapper is, we only attract the life that we put out in the universe. If we don't put our authentic selves out there, we aren't going to attract that authentic love with others that we so desperately want and deserve. The process we go through in order to find love is nothing more than looking for love as an emotion projected on us by others. We think if we can just *be* enough for someone, they will love us. That is the farthest thing from the truth, hunny. In fact, it is the complete opposite.

We can do better, and you will do better by the end of this book. Stop trying to construct the ideal love story in your head while looking in the mirror and whispering to yourself that your acne is making you ugly. Stop crying yourself to sleep because you didn't do enough for that stupid frat boy. Stop getting drunk in order to avoid the feelings of heartbreak you've experienced. Stop hating yourself and making yourself numb! Because at the end of the day, that is the person who is going to love you unconditionally for exactly who you are meant to be.

Dig inside yourself. What lessons did you learn from your failures? Why didn't it work out with Chad from the frat house or your first wife Stephanie? What did you fail to love about yourself, and so looked for validation within them? What type of love were you attracting by putting into the universe the failures you see in yourself? I bet if you were to start changing those failures today into positive lessons you can learn from, you'll start attracting those qualities you hold within yourself. You'll start to become heartbreak-proof because you'll start the process of healing within in order to see the beauty you hold. Try it. What's the worst that can happen?

CHAPTER 4

The Outsider Love ... and B.S.!

How many of you have heard the story of Cinderella? Cinderella lives in her attic sewing away, tending to her animals, and kind of hates her life. Yet, one magical day she gets swept off her feet when her magical fairy godmother comes and dresses her to the nines to send her to the Prince's Ball. With a glass slipper, some pixie dust, and love, Cinderella is taken away to live happily ever after. The End!

Except, this is real life, and unfortunately we don't have a "The End" title page or magic fairy dust (sorry). What we *do* have is a magical fairy godmother (me) who can help lead you to a life of being heartbreak-proof, and inadvertently toward your prince or princess! We just need to uncover one really, really big truth before I send you on your way. Now, this truth is the one that you probably are going to want to punch me in the mouth for, put your head under your pillow, and scream your little heart out while kicking your feet against your headboard. Oh, you don't do that? Well you might want to once I tell you the truth about finding your Prince Charming:

> Your charming love is only going to love you
> as much as you love yourself at the time.

I know I've already said this, but hey—sometimes you need things repeated a few different ways in order to fully understand them. So let's dive into it!

Once upon a time, I was dating this boy. I was a junior in college, freshly transferred to The College of Saint Rose for a new beginning, and taking Philosophy 101 (barf out loud). At the time I entered my Monday/Wednesday class, I was already overwhelmed and hating myself for a variety of reasons. I hated the fact that I dropped my one English class for a harder, higher-level one. I hated myself for wearing fabric shorts the first day, because obviously a cotton romper was so much more in style in 2016! I couldn't stand the fact that I shared with my first class that my "fun fact about me" was that I shared a birthday with my older brother (you know how college professors are). And I hated myself the most for attending my new college on the very first day hungover as frick. By 1:00 p.m., I had already run myself down about how I looked, my intelligence level, my capabilities, my decisions, the way I interested others, and about 2,976 other negative thoughts that popped into my head.

With a frown on and a pounding headache, I soberly walked to my class I dreaded the most in my schedule. I pushed open the door to reveal a classroom filled with students, and one seat open next to a tall blonde and directly in front of a tall, dark, and handsome boy. Picture the blush pouring into my cheeks. To spare you the deafening details of that wretched class, I'll skip to the part where Mr. Tall, Dark, and Handsome became my partner for the remainder of the semester for each group activity we had to do. Imagine the blush now! Guess who else was also in my group? Yup, the tall blonde. I took one look at her and thought, *Here is yet another girl I get to compete with for a guy's attention.* You see, back in 2016 everything was a competition to me when it came to the world of love. I wanted guys to think of me as all of the labels I had forced upon myself: pretty, smart, talented, interesting. However, my self-confidence was also a -300, and I could barely stand to look in the mirror at myself much less work up the courage to compete with tall, beautiful blondes. Hence, I was far from heartbreak-proof.

As the semester continued, Mr. Tall, Dark, and Handsome revealed to me that he had a girlfriend, and that said girlfriend was not making him happy. They had been together for a while, and he wasn't getting anywhere with her. We became friends, and before I knew it, I was swooning for him to pick me. You remember in gym class when you wanted to be picked for the dodgeball team? Yeah, that was me with being picked by any guy to be their girlfriend. Can you say "set up for a heartbreak"? Anywho, we grew closer, began texting, snapping, DMing on Instagram, and going ice-skating. He even came to some of the basketball games at school to watch me cheer! We were becoming incredibly close. At the end of our fall semester, he chose to break it off with his girlfriend in order to pursue me. FINALLY!

For about a month we continued to hang out, but our talks became more intimate. He disclosed the flaws he had seen in his ex-girlfriend, pointed out all of the ways she didn't satisfy him, and even said that he thought I could go above and beyond to make him the happiest he had ever been. Imagine the pressure that was put on me! Only, I didn't recognize it. Instead of taking a step back and realizing all of the expectations he was putting on me to be the perfect girlfriend, I let the expectations absorb me. I overanalyzed every word he said, internalized it, and began working on how to make myself the perfect girl to check off all of the boxes on *his* list.

The craziest part about it? I didn't even know I was doing this. I just thought I was stepping into a more genuine version of myself. The thing is, when we are searching for love from others, we take on their expectations of what love is supposed to look like. Don't get me wrong: it is 100% natural to have expectations of a relationship. That's the whole point of avoiding settling and becoming heartbreak-proof. However, we cannot perpetuate those expectations on others in order to love them or to gain their love. The purest forms of love happen out of genuineness.

I started changing myself by the way I acted. Mr. Tall, Dark, and Handsome was a bit on the negative side, what we like to call "Doom and Gloom." He was always finding something to hate about life. He was also extremely sarcastic, so I traded in my silly sense of humor for darker humor and edgy jokes. He enjoyed smoking pot with his friends, so I sucked up my asthma and decided to become a Bob Marley follower as well. He liked girls who were able to be calm, cool, and collected, so when he would flirt and go off with different girls whom he claimed were his "friends," I would silently cry in the corner of a party with people who were strangers to me. Since I had such low confidence in myself, I chose to conform to every expectation he had voiced to me, despite what I had wanted for him and myself. I would tell myself, *Well Hails, if you want him to like you …* or, *You can suck it up. He's a great guy.* By no means was Mr. Tall, Dark, and Handsome a bad guy or a good guy (remember, I hate labels), but he was someone who I felt I had to change for in order to receive his love. I didn't have enough love for myself, so the more I could be what he wanted me to be, the more he would give me. Right?

Although this relationship had me changing faster than Miley Cyrus into Hannah Montana (huge fan), not all of the changes were negative. One of the best changes I had undergone during this time was the transformation into who I was always destined to be. *Duh, duh, duh, duuuuuhhhhhh!* Remember when I told you I was your fairy godmother?

About three months into our relationship, Mr. Tall, Dark, and Handsome and I had experienced quite the turmoil for a new couple who was supposed to be in their honeymoon phase. We had numerous fights, there were many tears, lots of screaming, and about five potential breakups. Despite my best efforts to show him I was enough for him and everything he had longed for, I still wasn't meeting his expectations. It was St. Patty's Day 2017, and instead of hanging out with my friends on my cheering squad, he had convinced me to hang out with his friends in a basement. I know what you're thinking, but I promise this was a game changer! I knew that one of his closest friends was a medium, and I was extremely intrigued to hear what she had to say to me. I figured that night would be opportune as ever to learn what the world of the dead had to say!

After about three glasses of wine and lots and lots of dancing, I finally worked up the courage to ask her to read me. To my surprise, Gab turned to me and informed me that I was in fact a medium, and that I could read myself. WHHAATTTTT. I think my head literally spun around my body at that point. I argued with her for about an hour, and then finally gave it a try. Turns out, she was right! I read three other partygoers, predicted the future for two (which has come true), and validated messages I had been hearing from spirit for years. Although this was one of the most enlightening experiences I had ever had, it was also a dreadful one. I had been hearing from my own intuition for a while that Mr. Tall, Dark, and Handsome had a scorned soul, but I didn't believe myself. I had heard he was dark, hurting, empty, and manipulative at his core, but was well covered by his charming looks. I thought it was another distorted thought that arose from my overanalyzing. However, I learned that this particular message, along with about 5,000 others, was actually spirit trying to get through to me.

Despite hearing the message from spirit myself and through Gab, I still pushed forward with my relationship. Without a doubt, there were more tears, more backbending, and more pushing myself to my limits in order to get the love that I longed for. It wasn't until July of 2017 when things finally came burning down around me.

I had gone on vacation with my family in Florida, hesitant to leave Mr. Tall, Dark, and Handsome (mind you, we had just spent five days together with his family on a vacation to Vermont). I had a weird feeling as I left and could feel myself slipping away from him. Prior to going on the vacation in Vermont, Mr. Tall, Dark, and Handsome had revealed to me that he didn't believe in what I could do, nor did he think being a medium was a real thing. He informed me that he thought it was completely made up, and that I was just spreading messages of what people wanted to hear. Not only did he bash me down to the ground with those comments, he also put a cherry on top and said I was too positive and perky! Me? Perky? No way!

I was absolutely torn. I couldn't believe he had thought all of those things about me and my newfound passion, one that completed my soul beyond limits, which I didn't know was possible. For the first time in twenty years, I felt like a part of me, the real me, was finally showing through. And in a five-minute argument, I had lost my passion, my drive, and the only glimmer of love I had had for myself, ever. I decided that if I wanted love from him, I was going to have to give up being a medium. So, that is exactly what I (almost) did. I refused to book readings for the next two weeks since we were going on vacation. I stopped meditating, and I put a halt to bettering my practices. Thinking this would win him over, I shared with him my plan one night, to which I did not receive an answer. Nothing. Nada. Zip. Okay, I guess that's that then. HA. Not so fast.

Just when I thought I had gotten over a hurdle and I would return to New York from Florida tan, happy, and rejuvenated, Mr. Tall, Dark, and Handsome had some other plans. Around 9:00 p.m. the night my flight was departing from Florida, he decided to spill the beans that he was no longer in love with me, and that he was actually in love with his ex-girlfriend the entire time. Talk about deflating. I could not wrap my head around it. I was more hurt than ever. Not only had he bashed his girlfriend, but he filled my head with expectations that he said he was looking for in a girl. I gave those to him, and it turns out he wanted the original instead? Are you effing kidding me? I thought my head spun around on St. Patty's Day, boy was I mistaken. My heart was shattered into a million pieces. The one guy I felt I was making headway with, the one I had "evolved" for, the one who I had stepped into myself more than ever with, was leaving me high and dry, with a newfound passion, personality, and opportunity in my hands. Although the breakup sucked, I couldn't deny the possibilities that lay ahead for me without him.

I was depressed for about a week. I laid in bed crying silently, while Mom and Dad were overcome by joy that I had finally gotten the courage to leave Mr. Tall, Dark, and Handsome. Oh, how I used to love to leave out some details to spare myself uncomfortable situations. I hated him, I hated myself, and I hated everything about me that drove him away. I was in this constant cycle of bashing him for making me become this version of myself that I thought was ideal to him. After about a week's time, and with clarity through the power of intuition, I realized that it wasn't all his fault. Actually, it was barely his fault at all. So who's fault was it, you ask? Well, clearly it has to be someone's fault! There is always someone to blame for a relationship not working out! If it wasn't his fault, who was it? Ah, I see that finger pointing at me. So, on came another week of self-loathing, hatred, beating myself up for not seeing the red flags, not remaining true to myself, and of course not being *enough* for him.

I let myself bask in this disappointment for about a month after the breakup. At that point, I was returning to college for yet another year filled with promise, excitement, and most of all, boys! I told myself the week before I returned to college that this year was going to be different, and that I was going to fall for someone who I actually deserved. Someone who would give me their time in some fashion; someone who would look at me with awe. Someone who was athletic, cool, put together, and tall. Someone who was deemed as popular by the entire student body. Someone who would help me become somebody. I wasn't going to let them break my heart, gosh darn it!

Whoa, dramatic gasp. Post-breakup with Mr. Tall, Dark, and Handsome, I had a few epiphanies. For starters, I had to change my hair ... like yesterday. I realized that maybe part of the reason he left me for his ex was because my hair wasn't dark enough. So, I went to the salon to get some lowlights. Then, I realized that I didn't even want him back, because I was a badass bitch (no seriously, that's what I said to myself), and I wanted to become one of the girls that slept around and got attention from everyone. And I began to slowly realize that all I really wanted, more than anything in the world, was for a guy of higher social standing to recognize me and give me attention. Talk about shallowness.

Although I realized I was shallow in my desire for attention from an athlete supergod on campus, I also couldn't help but crave that love from such a person. I had grown up knowing the attention these types of people could get, and the attention I could also get if I was associated with them. I also knew the love they could give and I could give based on the expectations that surrounded the two of us. Yet again, I had fallen into the same cycle of wanting to match the expectations of someone else in order to attract their love. Cue the entrance of Mark!

Mark was the star of the Saint Rose basketball team and, to be completely transparent, the star of my life during my cheer days there. I was constantly stealing looks at Mark from across the court, with the desperate desire to get his attention, spark up a love story, and make the rest history. Let me make this real clear and real short for y'all—I was no more than a speck of dirt on Mark's Nike high-top basketball shoes. Nevertheless, I persisted on the journey of gaining his love and more importantly his attention over many months (or rather, years) while attending college.

While attempting and failing to win Mark over at games, the club, and on the green at school while throwing spirals with the football, I eventually realized I was starving not for Mark per se, but for his attention—imagine my shock! Although I hate to admit it, I didn't even really like Mark. Sure, he was appealing, standing at six foot four with bleached blond hair and a sparkling smile, but I didn't know him any more than I knew the Camelot sandwich guy who made my buffalo chicken panini every Tuesday (huge shout-out to him). To be honest, I was obsessed with obtaining his attention and affection just to say I got it. I wanted nothing more than to say I, Hali the cheerleader who was a nobody on campus, stole the heart of one of the most prestigious athletes on campus.

After an emotional rollercoaster of a chase with Mark, I finally landed a shot with him after a sloppy PSP night. For those of you not from the upstate New York area, PSP is the equivalent of going to a hometown party during your freshman year of college over Christmas break, getting far too drunk to function and waking up and hating yourself the next morning because you Cotton-Eyed Joe'd too hard to show the snobby girl from your pre-calc class senior year of high school who's boss. Take a moment to picture what this night looked like for me. Regardless, I was beyond stoked when my opportunity finally arose from the ashes of my embarrassment the moment Mark asked to go home with me. However, the excitement ended there, as that was the only highlight of the night.

Shortly after getting back to my apartment, I learned that Mark wasn't looking to have a soul-level conversation about how we were going to get married and remain college sweethearts long after the night. After all, he was a twenty-two-year-old athlete looking for what all college boys want, if you know what I mean. Talk about demoralizing. I was embarrassed, hurt, and beyond emotional. I mean, how could he not want to fall in love with me? Had I not made it clear as I stared him up and down from fifty feet away every day that I was looking for a relationship? You mean to tell me that I put out into the universe that I wanted *attention* from an athlete supergod from campus and that's all I got? Attention? Give me a break! How the heck is manifesting supposed to help anyone if it's taken so literally? Well, young Hails, that brings us to an important point of this chapter.

Let me back up real quick. As I mentioned before, I grew up in an extremely loving family with both of my parents at home, my two brothers, and my grandmother all at my disposal. By no means was I deprived from love and attention in the slightest. But, being the only girl of the family, I did receive love and attention in a different format than that of my brothers. My parents fawned over the boys' athletic abilities, whereas for me, they placed a larger emphasis on my intelligence. My brothers were regarded as popular by almost everyone in the school, whereas I was regarded as "Cori's little sister" or "Bailey's older sister." They were boys and could get away with sneaking out for a beer here and there, whereas I was expected to stay home and be a good little girl, with all of my priorities figured out.

From the earliest of times, we (me, along with many of you) were given certain expectations from outsiders that made us subconsciously internalize what we have to do in order for those around us to love us. The way we obtain attention is directly correlated to what we were envious of as children: the way we wanted to be, or the way we were just to match the expectations perpetrated onto us. The mere idea of us breaking these unspoken laws or lifestyles would repulse others, and make it so they don't love us anymore, right? WRONG! Unfortunately, I didn't realize this until I was done with college. Hopefully you find this message at a point in your life where you still feel willing and able to make a change about it!

I think the saddest part of the entire rollercoaster I had been on up until this point of my life was not the broken hearts or the hatred that was thrown from one person or the other. It wasn't the countless nights I had spent crying into my pillow over not being *enough*, and it wasn't the ten pounds I was rapidly gaining from each new scar a boy left on my heart. No. The saddest part was that with each new experience I had gone through that involved love, I told myself more and more that I didn't deserve love at all because of who I was. And I didn't even know who I was. I was living the same heartbreak over and over again, just to prove my point that boys will never like me enough to have me as their girlfriend.

I remember lying in bed and sobbing. I'm talking big old breaths in and out, screaming silently until the veins popped out of my head, asking God or Angels or whatever spiritual being you may believe in why I couldn't just have one person. Why was it that everyone around me, including the most rotten of them all, had a boyfriend? Yet, every boy that came into my life went running the other way? How many of you can relate to that? You see all of these other people in your lives getting married, getting pregnant, traveling the world with their boo thang, and you're sitting on the couch eating an entire pint of Ben and Jerry's peanut butter cup ice cream while binge watching *Friends* for the 18,000th time! How darn lame! Or at least, that's what I thought to myself every night when I was in that exact situation.

The truth of the matter is this—the thing I did "wrong" was not the guys I chose or the relationships I got into. It had nothing to do with me not deserving it, but everything to do with me being destined to go through those relationships to bring me to the exact point that I'm at right now. I was refusing to learn the lessons I was being taught in order to become heartbreak-proof; instead, I continued to review my flaws every few months to reinforce my idea that I was unlovable. I couldn't have one person love me, because the truth was, I didn't even love me. Lord, I couldn't even like me. Nor did I even know who "me" was. Sure, I knew I had brown hair and blue eyes, and my name at birth was Hali Claire Winch, I was a cheerleader and a college student and soon to be a teacher, but what did all of that really say about me? Who was I once I removed all of those labels? What made my blue eyes sparkle with passion? What made me curse like there was no tomorrow? What got me out of bed every morning, and inspired me to keep moving forward?

The hard truth was, I wasn't missing out on love because the universe didn't think I deserved it. Instead, I was missing out on love because the universe knew I needed to find it within myself first. Someone can only give you the love that you give yourself, and you can only love others as much as you love yourself. If your cup isn't full, how can you fill someone else's, and vice versa?

Love is a reciprocal act. Have you ever heard it takes two to tango? Two can't tango if one hasn't got their own dancing shoes. The love I wanted from other people couldn't be given to me with Mr. Tall, Dark, and Handsome or Mark or Jerry or Will, because it didn't exist yet. Sure, I had an idea of love and what went into it, but I didn't know what it was like to wake up every morning loving myself unconditionally for who I was. Let's not forget, I didn't even know who I was at twenty years old! It was unrealistic for me to expect any of them to love me, when there was barely a me there. Furthermore, I couldn't get mad at a guy for not loving me after I conformed to his expectations, but instead I realized that I didn't have my own expectations to live by. The love that comes from others has to come from you first. Fill up your own cup with whatever floats your boat! That is the only foolproof way that you can become heartbreak-proof.

CHAPTER 5

Labels

As mentioned—I am an intuitive medium. This is one of the many hats that I wear. But if I was to count—I wear, well, too many hats to actually count. The truth of the matter is, we all wear roughly a bazillion different hats throughout the span of our lives. I don't think I can make all of my hats fit in this one small book if I was to count all of them. Here's the thing with hats, though: they can be good, or they can be bad. Think of a fedora. Fedoras can be super cute, trendy, hell—even edgy if you have the right shirt to go with it! However, if my father wore one with his ripped BOCES t-shirt, starring some beautifully placed oil stains on his Wrangler jeans, that fedora may look a little scary. My point is, a hat, or label, may look good on one person, but it most definitely is not for every person. Labels ultimately lead us far away from becoming heartbreak-proof, especially when we put them on ourselves.

Think about yourself. If you were to think of five hats that you wear, what are the first five that come to mind? Okay, now think of your brother/sister or even best friend. Do they wear the same hats as you? More than likely, they probably don't. Some of us do have overlaps of hats with those we are closest with, but that does not mean that the label fits all. The problem we run into in this society is that we have this constant need to "fit a hat," or a label. When we describe ourselves to others or when we think about others describing us to strangers, these hats are the first thing to come to our minds. "She's a mother, nurse, funny girl, sweetheart, and rich." Barf. Well, not barf, but ... barf. I mean who wouldn't want to be described like that? I know I sure hope my brothers or friends describe me and my hats in such positive light to other people!

Here's the thing, though—yes, your hats do describe you. Kind of. Sure, they scratch the surface of what you are. But they don't tell someone *who* you are. They're not meant to. Labels are black and white. They're arbitrary based on who is using them. Labels are just ... labels. They're not necessarily a bad thing. After all, they give a pretty picture of who you are on the outside. The problem we run into with labels is sometimes (okay, a lot of times), we internalize these labels. *You mean I swallow that happy pill and I become happy because my mother told her BFFs at lunch that I am just the happiest eighteen-year-old alive?* Absolutely flipping not. Let me break this down for all of y'all, because it took me the longest time to bust through these suckers!

Labels are adjectives, job descriptions, titles, and personality traits that are given to us based on what others observe. They are more than likely subjective, as they are projected onto us based on how others feel when they are around us. Many times we give ourselves labels in order to fit in, or to, *duh, duh duh*, meet the expectations that are set forth for us. Like I said, labels aren't the bad guys here. We have to be able to use words to describe ourselves to employers, lovers, neighbors, the crazy lady whose house you accidentally show up to when you try to go on a date (ha ha ha, whoops). No worries, the old woman who answered the door that night was extremely kind and pointed me to door #2 of the townhouse after describing herself perfectly to me! We run into trouble with labels when they become more than how we describe ourselves—when they become who we are. Labels are excellent 2D photos of ourselves. You can look your future boss in the eye while your knees are shaking and you feel yourself peeing a little bit, saying that you have integrity, a strong work ethic, and you get along great with others. Those labels may describe you, but they aren't you. You are the person that created those labels, not the other way around. By showing up to work ten minutes early every day, doing your workload, telling your boss that you just can't complete another work order today because you are already overloaded, and that Peg-with-a-smug-smile can do it for another back pat is who you are. The labels help to describe those actions that make you *you*. Not the other way around.

Let me give you an example. One of my most famous labels I have given myself over the years is *teacher*. I have been a "teacher" since I was able to talk. My parents used to tell me I was a teacher, I told myself I was a teacher, my own teachers told me I was a teacher. It was basically embroidered on my heart from the time I was born. I can remember going into my basement and lining my dolls up on the floor while I taught them their ABCs and 1,2,3s. It was in my blood. It was who I was destined to be. That was it. Nothing else other than a teacher.

In my senior year of high school, I had an amazing opportunity to work with teachers in my elementary school who taught me the ropes of teaching. They taught me how to grade papers, organize desks, have effective behavior management ... the whole nine yards. I even remember some of them giving me small groups to read books with or to give a spelling test. Easy peasy lemon squeezy!

I entered college my freshman year knowing that education was going to be a breeze. After all, I was a natural-born teacher and could do that bologna in my sleep! Boy, was I knocked off my high horse my first day of education classes. Lesson plans? Differentiation? Teaching to the Zone of Proximal Development? Cognitive, physical, social, and emotional needs? Maslow who? Piaget what? Needless to say, I returned home my first day of freshman year with eyes filled with tears and a heart that was beyond broken. How could something I had identified myself as for so long feel so hard? Wasn't I already a teacher? All I had to do was friggin' show up! I was yet again heartbroken.

I remember driving home that night from my first day of classes at Hudson Valley Community College. I was beyond lost on the vocabulary terms they were throwing around, not to mention I was overwhelmed by the amount of hard work, dedication, and passion that was needed to teach children. That day was the first time I recognized that just because I gave myself the label of teacher, didn't mean I *was* a teacher. You see, we aren't our labels. We are how we are. The labels just help describe us, but labels do not define us. We are defined by our actions, our morals, and the way we live our lives. We are what we bring to the table, the way we treat others; the ways in which we interact with those we surround ourselves with. Yes, labels help give parameters to help us find our way in this world, but they are by no means the end-all be-all of who we are.

After coming to the realization that I actually needed to work in order to become a teacher, I made the decision to do what it took. I learned how to write a lesson that could reach the minds of twenty-five diverse learning abilities. I learned how to teach a young child to stay engaged for more than two minutes. I learned that teaching goes beyond just teaching academics, but instead encompasses teaching children to keep their hands to their own bodies, how to make a friend, how to overcome obstacles. I learned how to respond to a child when they tell me to "Screw off," or that their parent was brought to prison in front of them last night.

I learned that even though a student knows that 2+2=4 on Monday, it doesn't mean on Tuesday they will remember. I learned that your lesson probably won't happen, and you have to be able to roll with the fact that little Johnny interrupted your lesson on poetry to tell you that songs speak to him more, that he is able to connect with lyrics in a way that teaches him more about rhyme, similes, and metaphors than a Robert Frost poem ever could. I learned that academics take the back seat when a child doesn't know how to regulate their emotions. I learned that sometimes your boss can be a real pain in the ass, but you have to just push through because you have to do what's best for the kids, not what's best for you. I observed, I sat back, I practiced, I studied. After four-and-a-half years and six teacher certification exams, I became that *teacher* I had always labeled myself as. Or so I thought.

It was my first day of student teaching. Finally—it was time to show what I've learned and teach the youngins about Social Studies and Science. Whoop whoop! I was so excited to be teaching in Albany. My kids were awesome, my supervisor was hysterical, and my cooperating teacher was top of the line! I couldn't have asked for a better placement. Things went pretty smoothly, and I was asked to implement my first unit on Indigenous People. Can you say yikes? So, I threw together a PowerPoint slideshow with videos, created a Google Classroom filled with resources, found artifacts that supported what we were learning about, and brought it all together by having the students create a research project to show their knowledge. For the most part, it was a success. The kids enjoyed the project, they all did well, and I got some pats on the back with *You are a wonderful teacher, Hali!* Gulp. I remember my heart squeezed with anxiety in the moment I heard that label.

I remember looking at the faces of the twenty-three wonderful students I was instructing. They were young, with lives ahead of them. They had a few labels slapped on them, but not many. They weren't told from the time they were three that they were great teachers. No, instead, that was me. I had studied and persevered for years, for this is what I was destined to be. That was who I was. I was a teacher, and I would be a teacher forever.

That thought scared the living daylights outta me. I had about eight million questions run through my head in an instant. How would I do this for the rest of my life? How many years could I teach children about Indigenous People? How would I make a living off of a teacher's salary? What things can I not do now that I am considered a teacher? Can I no longer go out and get drunk at PSP because I might run into a student's parents? Holy Toledo, Batman. I was merely twenty-one, and I was having a midlife crisis.

This is the trap we get into with labels. Once we get them, we feel we're stuck with them. Not only that, but we feel they are the only hat we can wear for the rest of our lives: that's it, we have them for life. This is true not only for work positions, but personality traits, looks, and skill sets. We get in this vicious mindset that if someone gives us the label, it is true and it is unchanging. We are stuck being that ugly, fat, lazy, unmotivated, selfish, or cute, funny, smart, teacher's pet, teacher for the rest of our lives. Unfortunately, when we get into this mindset, we see nothing but devastation, fear, and anxiety for ourselves. Ultimately, this leads to self-loathing and us breaking our own hearts. Hence, labels can also be not the greatest thing for us.

I can remember going back to my dorm the night that I had received that wonderful compliment from my supervisor and cooperating teacher and having a full-blown anxiety attack. Of course, that was a compliment that I had wanted to receive. It was exactly what I had felt I needed to be a "good teacher." I needed the approval of other people (a.k.a. I needed to meet their expectations of what a good teacher was). But what if I didn't end up being a teacher? What if I wanted to be more, do more? What if I woke up tomorrow and I wanted to do something in business? Or I couldn't teach sixth grade math? What would I be then? What would my label turn into? Or even worse—would those who gave me that label be disappointed because I was no longer fitting into who they thought I was?

You may have found yourself in this same situation. Maybe you define yourself by what you do for work. Or maybe you define yourself as a mother, father, brother, sister. Maybe you define yourself as kind or sweet. Whatever the label is that you give yourself, you're scared to break away from it for fear of what others may begin to think of you. I mean, what would happen if you went away with your girls for the weekend instead of staying home and cleaning up toys or washing the dishes while simultaneously holding a kid and feeding everyone else dinner? Or can you imagine what would happen if for two seconds you stop being the masculine man who can fix everything and never shows emotion, and instead you fall in love with reading a "girly" book like this to learn to love yourself?

God forbid we break the labels that we not only put on ourselves, but also those that everyone else puts on us.

Well, here's the good news: you are more than your label. Remember, those labels we have are just a way to describe ourselves. It is NOT how we define ourselves.

Back when I was having my crisis of being stuck with the label "teacher" forever, I didn't know how to handle the situation. I thought my only two options were to either be the teacher forever, or quickly change my career path as soon as possible to show everyone I was more than my one job. Yes, that would do it! (As k me how happy my parents were when I told them this grand idea ... NOT).

I immediately hopped onto my computer, looked up grad programs, and before midnight that night, I had applied to the Speech and Language Pathology Graduate Program at Saint Rose. Whew. I could wipe my brow that night knowing that I was going to sleep with the possibility of changing my label of teacher!

To my surprise, I actually got into the program! It took numerous interviews, references, and many, many bottles of wine, but I did it! I would begin attending Speech Grad School in December 2019! That will show everyone! Little did I know the heartbreak that was about to ensue.

It was when I sat down with my graduate admission advisor that I realized the mistake I had made. Not only did I just switch from one label to another, but I had adversely added another four years of schooling to my already crazy-busy plate! Okay, okay, it's cool. Everything was fine. Thankfully, he talked me off of a ledge and told me that I would be okay, my grades were more than satisfactory, and that the program wouldn't be as much textbook knowledge as it would be life-application knowledge. Phew. I thought I was in the clear after sweating profusely for twenty minutes. That was until the dreaded question came out of his mouth; *Hali, why do you actually want to do speech? What is going to make you get out of bed every morning in order to show up and do your job?* Cue the song "Heartbreaker" by Pat Benatar.

Damn. Talk about a bus hitting you. The truth was, I didn't know the first thing about speech therapy, other than I was still a bit bitter that I never received any in elementary school. That stuff looked as fun as recess when I was in second grade! After a few moments of not responding, my advisor asked me again, *What is it that makes you want to do speech instead of education?* I sat for a moment, and I gave the answer that spoke to my intuition. I told him that rooting for the underdog was who I was. Whether I was five or twenty-one, I always wanted the underdog to kick life's ass. I wanted to be the biggest supporter of the person who everyone in their life deemed as a failure. I wanted to be the smiling face that made them remember why they were put on this Earth. I wanted to be the person who gave a child a voice, who helped them to figure out their purpose. I wanted to be that role model, the guidance they need, and the one who shows them their abilities. I wanted to be there for them, and to show up when nobody else did.

As the words came out of my mouth, I realized one of the most important lessons I have yet to learn in my short twenty-four years of life. I wasn't a speech pathologist. Christ, I wasn't a teacher. I wasn't a good person, or a bad person. I wasn't super, great, or even phenomenal. I wasn't the meaningless labels I had been giving myself my whole life.

Instead, I am my heart. I am my passion. I am my desires, my dreams, my ideas. I am the thoughts that come to me at two a.m. when I can't sleep. I am the sparkle that comes to my eyes when I help people realize who they are. I am the person who others in life can count on. I am the hugs and kisses I give my family, and the smiles I give out to strangers. I am more than the labels that define my existence. Instead, my existence is who I am. It was on this day that I was given the first glimpse of how to become heartbreak-proof by becoming myself unbound by labels.

Think about it: strangers don't know you. Some people in your life don't know you. The only person who knows you, is you. The labels that others use to describe you is the most simplistic form of who you are. They describe the surface level of your personality, your looks, and your actions. Labels are perceptions and impressions that are portrayed to others. But who you are is completely within you. How you act, what you think, or what lights you up inside are the attributes you need to strive to love about yourself. Forget the labels of kind, caring, compassionate, pretty, smart, driven, or hard-working. What actions do you do each and every day that you are proud to do? What people come into your life who make you feel good? What hobbies do you have that you cannot imagine your life without? What passions light a fire in your soul? Those are what make you heartbreak-proof.

You see, those qualities are who you are. They are what make you, you. And you want to know the best part about them all? They are uniquely you. Just like your fingerprint, inner parts of you are unique. Not one person on this Earth is cut from the same cloth as you (thank Jesus!). We make up one entire being. God, spirit, Buddha, or whatever higher power you believe in gave you qualities that you can appreciate within yourself. You weren't born into this world with labels (other than maybe a gender). So why start putting them on yourself now to fit in with the rest of the world? Why not let the inner you write your own story?

Show people who you are through the way you act, the thoughts you have, the ideas that come out of you. We live in a world where expectations are innate and labels are unavoidable. However, we're lucky.

Labels help us get perspective on how we show ourselves to others. When we're given labels, we're given a sense of feedback. Think about it. Has anyone ever given you the label "bitch"? What about "jerk"? I know I'm raising my hand high! Or even better, "psycho"? When I was given these labels, frankly, I was hurt. I couldn't imagine what I had said, done, or not done in order to receive such a hateful label from someone. But that's just it: it was a label. It was not who I was. These labels gave me a chance to reflect, though. Why did Nicole in twelfth grade call me, a freshman, a bitch? Was I acting like a bitch? I don't think I had even spoken a word to her, to be honest! The deeper I began thinking about it, though, I thought about actions I had recently taken toward others, or to myself. Hurtful words I may have spoken about her friends or even her family.

Although I didn't enjoy the label "bitch" she had so kindly slapped on me, my homegirl had a point. I wasn't being as genuine as I knew I was. I knew on the inside I was a person who thrived on seeing others happy. So why in tarnation did I tell that girl in the gym that her shirt and shorts didn't match? I mean, whose shorts and shirt actually did match in freshman gym, anyway?

I was getting my heart broken by others because I wasn't being true to myself or listening to who I was. Instead, I was putting up a front in order to impress others, which ultimately led to negative labels being used on me. It was through labels like this that I realized there were some areas of myself that I could improve. Now, by no means does every label someone gives you have a rhyme or a reason. No way, no how. However, sometimes they are a good way to get us to stop and think.

Really think—was this label given to me because I wasn't being myself? Or maybe I was being myself, but I don't really like that version of me. Maybe that label brought to the surface an issue that you've been working to cover up for a while now. Or maybe the label brought to light the desire in you to be yourself, love yourself more. After all, the truer you are to yourself, the more heartbreak-proof you become to others.

Yes, labels are lame. I hate giving myself labels, and I hate labeling others. However, they are a part of life, and they are a necessity. My point about labels is, you can't get wrapped up in defining yourself just by the labels you give yourself and are given by others. So much goes into you. You are more than just a couple of words used to describe you. Remember, you are what you make of yourself. If you don't like the labels that others put on you, but you feel that they have some semblance of truth, you have the power to change them. The fact of the matter is, you have to be the one who loves you for you at the end of the day. Don't forget that this is all about how to love yourself at a soul level. So are you ready for another challenge?

Try thinking of different labels that you have either given yourself over the years, or ones that others have given you. Write them down in your journal, on your phone, or speak them aloud. After you do that, think about the qualities within yourself that make up those labels. For example, "Mom." What makes you a mom, other than having kids that came out of your you-know-what? Is it your love for them? Is it your drive to give them the most incredible life possible? Is it your desire for structure, balanced with a fun life-style? What in you makes that label true? If you come to a label you don't particularly enjoy, what is it that you don't enjoy about it? Is it that on some level there's something in you that makes it true? What can you do for yourself to change it?

The most important part of this challenge is to make changes that make you feel *good*. We focus so much of our time and energy on making others like us, measuring up to the expectations put in front of us, looking good on the outside. Often, we let the inside get ugly, which sets us up for failure in the eyes of others and ourselves. Take the time to make it pretty. Dig deep within yourself, and think about what makes you, you. Think of those passions, those desires, the things that light your eyes up and make you flash a big old smile. Write down the things you enjoy doing, the people you enjoy being with, and the parts of you that make you proud. Keep adding to this list. Keep reminding yourself that you are so good. You are a light in this world, and you are unique to it. You bring your own set of amazing attributes to the table that deserve to be recognized and celebrated within you, by you. Take the day or night to do this. Fall in love with yourself and make yourself that much more heartbreak-proof despite the labels.

CHAPTER 6
Let's Break Up ... with Ourselves.

If you're like me, you think you've been here many, many, many times. This "breakup," as I like to call it, is when you call it quits with yourself. This looks like (for me) binge-eating all of the Oreos, laying down and taking a nap instead of doing kickboxing, looking in the mirror and crying based on what I see, beating myself up for a text I sent to a guy. You get the picture.

The point is, we've all had these breakups with ourselves. Many times it's for something we do, say, or even think. In some cases, it is based on labels or expectations that are projected onto us by others. Whatever the form, it is miserable. But I'm here to tell you that breakups are good. Oh, they're oh-so-good. They're honestly one of the best things we can do for ourselves. We just suck with breakups because, ya know, we're humans. But what if I told you that breakups are what make us heartbreak-proof? Honestly, in my opinion, we need breakups in order to become the version of ourselves that can't be heartbroken over others. So, this chapter is dedicated entirely to breakups, and pushing past the stage of a breakup that many of us get to and stop at. I'm here to make you heartbreak-proof, remember?

Think about your latest breakup. If you've been married, think about your breakup prior to your marriage. There were things that caused you to get to that point. Maybe your significant other was rubbing you wrong on a daily basis. Maybe you had eyes for someone else who was kinder, more intelligent, a harder worker, or even more attractive. Maybe you were getting out of a relationship that was not the best for you, physically or mentally. Whatever it is, you went through the breakup for a reason.

It may have been hard for you to identify that reason right off the bat, though. Often when we break up with someone, we have feelings of regret, guilt, confusion—you name it. Several emotions go through our heads until we eventually make a choice; meaning, we choose to move back, stay still, or move forward. Let's throw our feet up on the ottoman and dive a little deeper into these, shall we?

Move back. Ah, yes. Undoubtedly we have all been here at one time or another, whether it was with a significant other, a friend, or maybe even a crush! In terms of a breakup, a move back is when you quite literally move back. This could be you going back to the person who hurt you, returning to old habits that comforted you, or even diving deeper down the rabbit hole of self-pity and despair. Now, going back isn't as bad as it sounds. To be frank, going back is necessary in some scenarios. Let me put on my intuitive medium hat for this one.

It is my belief as a medium that we all have old wounds that we are born into this lifetime with (kind of like the idea of reincarnation), as well as soul wounds we acquire throughout our time here on Earth. These wounds are a part of our souls that we experience that often don't have time to heal or are avoided. The unfortunate part for us is, we carry these wounds into our current lifetimes, and they subconsciously have an effect on how we see ourselves and the way in which we live our lives. In terms of a relationship, you may find that throughout your life you have been attracted to the same type of man (my hand is high in the sky right now). I figured out quickly that not only did I have a particular physical attraction to a certain type of man, but I also had a soul connection to men based on my wounds that I was carrying around with me. As you can probably tell from the previous chapters, I tended to go after guys that were a bit on the stand-offish side, noncommittal, indecisive, misogynistic—you get the picture. But, they also had the charm, wit, and charisma that drew me in.

Anyway, after years of less-than-spectacular relationships and continuously returning to the same "type" of guy over and over again for it to only end in heartbreak, I decided to take a deeper look into myself. About six months after determining that I was in fact an intuitive medium, I chose to sit and meditate on my current situation with men. I would ask my angels and my guides why it was I was attracting men who couldn't give a rat's nest about me, and what I was doing wrong to make them run the other way. After several failed attempts (or so I thought) of not receiving the answer, I chose to turn to my friend for help. At the same time, she was studying past life regressions, which is the way we can travel back within our souls to past lifetimes that we have lived. I can remember doing a past life regression and feeling anger, insecurity, and fear. There were countless emotions that I continued to repeatedly run into through the numerous past lives I witnessed. The one constant I realized was that in all of my lives, including this one, I was constantly looking for validation from others to ensure that I was enough.

From the time I was little, I was looking to my parents for their stamp of approval on whatever I chose to do. This ranged from sports performance, to school grades, to even the people I chose to hang out with. As I got older and entered the dreaded middle and high-school years, I found myself looking to friends and boys to provide that validation for me. I needed to hear compliments from them. I killed to catch someone checking me out. I always wanted to be the one who was noticed for her efforts or outfit. Eventually, as I got to the dating world, the same need of validation from others was projected to my significant others. I would conform to their labels and their expectations in order to feel validated by them. I wanted to dress in a way they thought was "pretty" or act in the way that they thought was "funny," even if it was untrue to who I was at my core.

I wish I could say it was easy, but this was probably one of the hardest demons I had to tackle in my lifetime. My need and desire for validation and attention needed to be tackled if I ever wanted a shot of becoming heartbreak-proof. However, at the age of twenty, I was unsure of how to tackle it. I didn't want to go back to some of the most dreaded memories of my life to uncover that I did what I did, or said what I said because I wanted the validation of someone to like me. It hurt too much to go back to those memories or those wounds that I had carried for so long to admit that I was doing it for others to like me.

It took me far longer than it should have, which is what led me to continue to move back. I continued to choose the same guys over and over again. I continued to binge-eat and cry when I gained a pound or five. I was on this constant hamster wheel of returning to what was comfortable and what I knew because it was easier than actually moving back to tackle the skeletons that were in my closet.

Moving back, at its core, is useful. It has its purpose, and its purpose is to help us realize the lessons we need to learn in order to heal and make it right. The past and current emotions that I had encountered made me realize that I had wounds of rejection, not measuring up, and never being enough. I carried all of those invisible wounds within my soul throughout this lifetime, which subconsciously made me choose guys who made me feel validated at a surface level. I was subconsciously creating habits such as binge-eating that made me feel validated in the moment, because it was easier than going back and finding out why I was eating what I was eating.

Moving back is just as important as moving forward in a breakup. Moving back allows us to peer deeper into our souls. We can begin to explore what it is that is pulling us in and making us choose the same person, relationship, or habit over and over and over again. However, the key to moving back is identifying the why. What is causing you to do that? Is it because you actually like that habit or person, or is it what is comfortable? Do you have demons in the closet that you are refusing to let out if you move forward, so it's just easier to move back? You need to be able to address these questions in an honest manner in order to truly be able to get to the best part of the breakup cycle.

Stay still. The saddest part for me is, I see so many people "stuck" here. This is the part of a breakup where we identify those skeletons, but we choose to do nothing about them. The stay-still part of the cycle is very similar to that of the move back, but it is not as detrimental. In terms of a relationship, you stay still when you refuse to better yourself. You recognize your areas needing some love, but you refuse to do the work to get there.

For me, it was when I saw I was choosing men based on the validation piece, but instead of self-healing, I chose to continue looking for validation in other people. This included friends, family members, and of course, men.

Staying still occurs in our lives. When I found out that I was carrying wounds from my childhood and past lives that were affecting my current life on Earth, I didn't know what to do. I was overwhelmed by the fact that I had work to do, as well as confused on how to even heal my wounds. My old hurts resonated with me because they were not exactly comfortable, but they were familiar. I was conscious that I was picking guys who validated me, but I didn't know what the opposite was. Nor did I know how to counteract that feeling or need.

So, instead of getting help, I chose to sit where I was in my life. For me, I chose to avoid relationships. I decided to become emotionless, and I chose not to care what other people thought of me. I slept with randos, and I found feeling through sex. It was easy. Except, it wasn't. I found myself wondering what the guy of the night thought. Did he like it? Was I good? I was still in the same frame of mind where I needed validation in order to feel good about myself.

Quick story time to give you a better understanding of this stage: When I was six years old, I went swimming in my grandparents' pool. It was a beautiful August day, and I had the compelling thought that I was a majestic mermaid of the Pacific Ocean. I let my brown hair out of my ponytail and let it whirl in the pool as I flipped and twirled through the water. God, I was having the time of my flipping life. That was, until Bailey, my youngest brother, decided it was his friggin' turn to jump into the pool with his mouth wide open! I remember coming up above the water and seeing blood all around me. My poor mom went ghost white, and she was yelling to my grandfather to grab his handkerchief to stuff in my head. I was beyond confused because I thought we had just bumped heads. That was until I reached up to feel the gaping hole in my forehead. It was not a good afternoon, to say the least. But what does this have to do with staying still?

Well, I stuffed the handkerchief in my head and was rushed to the hospital by my wonderfully terrified parents. Upon arrival, I had the understanding that the doctors would look at my head, probably clean the wound, and send me on my merry way home. Nope. Boy, was I off the mark with that one. Instead, that told me to lay still while they forcibly held me down on the table and prepared to stitch up my head with eighteen gosh-darn stitches! Imagine my shock when I heard those bitches! God, I was scared. I remember kicking and screaming and telling the nurses, "NO!" I remember screaming for my dad to come hold me, and I believe I even tried to bite the one poor nurse who was trying to wipe blood from my forehead.

As minutes passed and the room cleared out, I eventually calmed down enough for a nurse to come in and clean my wound. I remember her wiping my blood away as she spoke so calmly to me. She was commenting on my beautiful blue eyes that stood out against my tan skin. She was talking to me about how I was the first good case to come into the emergency room that day with a solid wound to look at. She asked how the wound was created, and my mom re-explained the story, but forgot to mention I was doing it to be a mermaid. The nurse probably thought I was lame. Anyway, just as the nurse turned away from me, looking as if she was going to leave, she turned back and showed me a scar on her arm. The scar was enormous. I remember it going the entire length of her arm, and god, was it scary. She told me she doesn't normally show patients her scar, but she felt like I could handle it.

After showing her incredible mark, she told me the story of how she obtained the wound. I don't recall the exact details, but I can remember it was from when she hit a tree during an accident. She had blacked out when it happened, and all she remembered was being at home and people telling her to go to the hospital to get her stitches, but she didn't. She screamed at them, cried, and threw a fit. She wanted to stay right where she was, and she didn't want to stitch up her new wound. Fifteen years after the accident, she still had a large scar that reminded her every day of her horrific accident. I'll never forget the words she spoke to me: *I never healed my wound the way it was supposed to be healed. I just pretended like it didn't happen.*

Eighteen years later, and that nurse's story still resonates with me. I ended up getting the stitches, and now all I have is a small scar of teeth marks on my forehead that are hardly noticeable without pointing them out. I chose in that moment when I was six to heal my wound the right way. Despite wanting to stay still like the nurse had chosen, I needed to move forward and heal the wound that was in front of me. I remember this conversation often when it comes to healing my wounds. Many times we get stuck in our own minds. This could be with thoughts we have of ourselves or others, or it could be in the way we interact with others. We all have wounds that cause us to think and act the way we do. Thankfully, we have much more positive qualities than negatives, but it is the negatives that we get stuck on. We think that by ignoring them or avoiding them that we are moving forward, but instead, we are standing still.

I think of the *People Mover* ride at Walt Disney World. You stand on this track that moves below you. All around you, the scenery changes and you experience different settings filled with beautiful sights and people. But you are standing in the same spot. This is what happens when we fail to recognize and heal our wounds that are holding us back. Life goes on, days, months, and years pass. People come and go throughout our lives. However, we stand still. We aren't changing. We remain stagnant. We continue to learn the same lesson over and over and over again without changing the outcome. My professors in college used to say, *You can't expect a child to learn the lesson if the outcome is always the same.* That's exactly what happens when we stand still. This is one of the scariest things for me to experience with people. We are born into this world to adapt, to change with the world around us, and to learn. We are not meant to stay in the same job, the same relationships, the same houses and towns for our entire lives. We need to change and learn in order to make a life worth living. When we stand still, we are letting our lives pass us by without truly getting the full experience and outcomes we desire.

It took me years to get to the point where I was done just standing still. It wasn't until I was twenty-three, when I had hit rock-bottom after the worst year of my life, that I chose to actually make a change. I consciously chose to face those wounds head on, and figure out what I could do to heal them and change my outcome. I looked up ways to meditate and work on healing soul fragments and wounds. I sought help from my dearest friend Gab to take me through hypnosis and energy healing to help cure my demons.

By no means was it fun. To be honest, it was the last thing I ever wanted to do. I had to not only relive the memories that were the hardest to endure when they happened, but I had to re-experience the emotions that came with them, too. Standing still was no longer an option for me, though. I couldn't continue to live my life in this state of hatred, pity, and miserableness.

It breaks my heart to see so many I love to go through this on the daily just because they are standing still. They're watching their lives pass by without knowing how to heal their wounds. If this resonates with you, know that it is okay if you are currently standing still. The best part of the breakup cycle is that it comes in phases, and we get to choose which one we are in. We have that control! So, if you are feeling like this is you and you want to take control in order to move to the next phase of your life and become heartbreak-proof, keep reading for the best part yet!

Moving forward. Ah, the most blissful stage of all. Achieved by some, reached by many. This is the stage I am going to place the largest focus on, as I firmly believe it is the phase in which most of our life should be spent. Now, don't get me wrong. Staying still is a good place to be in order to enjoy the moments that life has to offer, but ultimately we never achieve the life we want if we continuously stay in that stage. So, let's begin, shall we?

In terms of the breakup phase, this is the stage when you actually make a conscious choice of action. In terms of relationships, this is the point where, obviously, you move forward and become heartbreak-proof. This could be in the way of finding someone new, finally starting a program that will help regain control of your mental health, or maybe it's joining the gym and getting a personal trainer. However, the catalyst of this phase is you make the conscious choice to take an action that helps *you*. This is the phase when we begin to heal our souls at a deeper level. We develop the standards we want in a relationship, we make lifelong choices that will benefit our health and well-being, and we go toe to toe with our hidden demons and covered-up traumas. This is the point in our lives that we stop choosing to live in the shadow of our ego, but instead take life by the balls and run with it. When I work with clients, they tell me this is the scariest phase of all, but worth the journey beyond measure. I promise you this—moving forward is the phase where your life begins.

Story time (again)! When I broke up with my high-school boyfriend Jerry, I went through the other two stages quite dreadfully. My initial reaction was to move forward right off the bat. Easy enough, right? The relationship was over and there was no attraction there, so moving forward would be easy. I would just snap other guys, message them, hang out whenever I wanted. Oh yeah, moving forward was going to be a breeze.

Oh, what a naive thought. Turns out, after a week of being single, I realized that it wasn't as easy as sending a guy a message and him being at your beck and call and hopping into another relationship. Oh god, no. Instead it consisted of me snapping guys and being left unread, being too scared to text other guys because of what they may think, and above all refusing to hang out with other guys because I would feel too awkward to talk to them. Instead of moving on and forward, I ended up moving backward. For me, that looked like reaching back out to Jerry and seeing if he wanted to spark up our love once more. When he shot me down, I was absolutely devastated.

I spent what felt like months obsessing over the idea that he no longer wanted me. I was constantly checking his Twitter feed for any and all inclinations that he was thinking of me, and referring to his snap score to see how much it increased every day (come on, some of you have done that, too). For lack of a better word, I was going neurotic trying to keep up with him, to the point that I lost sight of where I wanted to go myself. Months on end, I continued this vicious cycle of moving back to Jerry with no luck of moving forward. Finally in July, my best friend was sick of the pity I was giving myself, and chose to sit me down for the largest slap in my face I had yet to experience at that point in my life. Jerry had moved forward with someone new. Talk about a gut-wrenching feeling. I remember playing the whole conversation off as no big deal, and thinking that I would just now move on myself. Only it didn't work like that. Oh no, instead I moved to the staying-still phase. Cue the old T-Swift albums about boy drama.

Although I understood that Jerry had a new girlfriend and my fears were now present, I had no clue how to move forward. I had no clue how to find someone new, let alone even know if I had interest in someone other than Jerry. He had been my life for years, and now I was just supposed to ... stop? It made no sense to me. I had absolutely no clue what I wanted or what I was attracted to. I had no inclination of what standards I had when it came to men or how I wanted to be treated by them. I was in a stand-still stage. Day in and day out, I avoided my emotions about the situation I found myself in, reveled in my self-pity, and ultimately did nothing. I continued to message new guys and even talked to a few who became flings, but nothing serious. I still continued to look in the mirror on the daily and be haunted by what I saw. I refused to address my lack of self-love and chalked it up to the typical breakup mentality that we all go through. Newsflash—you hopefully won't have to go through it, because you'll be heartbreak-proof.

Eventually, I met a new guy who I became overly absorbed with, and I thought that just maybe I was finally moving forward. After all, I had a new guy who was extremely gorgeous, successful, and best of all, older than I was! My initial thought was, "Amen, finally a guy with some maturity! What could go wrong?" Sure, I still hated how I looked naked, and I dreaded talking about my past, but who cares! This guy seems to really like some part of me enough to spend time with me. Yeah, well all good things came to an end about six months after they started. I again went through the moving-back and staying-still phases, with a false thought that I was moving forward with love because I was dating new guys. Boy, was I wrong.

To tell you the god's honest truth, many times we think we move on when we find a new relationship and someone new to love us. I'm here to say that is not the case. Now, by no means am I saying that some of you who are in relationships right now are going to fail because you didn't properly move forward. Absolutely not. In fact, I have seen many cases where people are involved in long-term relationships and they are able to move forward within their relationship. However, you and your partner have to be willing to grow with one another. I will get into that in a second. For now, I want to focus more keenly on the idea of moving forward within ourselves.

Jerry and I called things quits back in 2016. It is now 2020, and I am finally moving forward. I am currently single, the healthiest I have ever been, fully and completely in love with myself, and best of all, I know how not to get my heart broken by looking for validation within myself instead of others. However, it took me years of understanding what moving forward actually was in order to do it. You see, I was stuck in the staying-still stage for a very long time. For the longest time, I refused to identify the demons in myself that were preventing me from loving myself and even receiving the love that I wanted. I had countless expectations for others and standards I wanted friends, family, and even lovers to measure up to, but I failed to have some expectations for myself. I was finding myself eating garbage, refusing to work out, doing crash diets, sleeping with random guys, putting myself out in order to get attention I was striving for, getting aggravated at friends for being flaky and ditching me when they caught a glimpse of my personality they didn't love. I was continuously putting the blame on other people *for years*. That was until I started dating Dave.

Dave will have a completely separate chapter dedicated to him, but to give you the gist, he is and always will be the second-greatest love of my life. Dave has been a part of my life starting in the tenth grade and stretching until adulthood, but ultimately he has been someone who has been an anchor to me. He is truly a blissful person who I am forever grateful for, and it was because of him that I am here writing this book for you. As mentioned, Dave has been a great friend of mine for about ten years. He was Jerry's best friend in high school, and ultimately someone who I had a keen eye for back in the day. Years passed and nothing happened between us, but over the summer of 2019, we chose to allow ourselves to explore each other past the boundaries of friends, and lo and behold, lots of love was held between us. However, I began to run into my demons that I could no longer ignore.

I began recognizing all of the negative self-talk I was doing—the way my weight was affecting my confidence, my sex life, and my social life. I noticed how my perseverating thoughts were ruling my days to the point that I couldn't get out of my own head to enjoy the moments I was a part of. I realized that ghosts from my past lives were haunting my current soul. This included fears I couldn't explain in regard to trusting others due to betrayal, obsession with others to the point I couldn't let them go, and control over food, time, and other's thoughts. I learned through meditation and energy healing sessions that these were attachments from lives I lived during the Holocaust, the AIDS pandemic, and early colonialized America. As a result, I had a wounded soul that impacted my daily functioning. I was beginning to run into obstacles daily that made life harder to live, and even worse, they were inhibiting my relationship with Dave from working. As hot and fast as the romance with Dave came to fruition, it left just the same. By November, he had ghosted me and was no longer in my life.

Now, I had been ghosted numerous times before, but this was different. Everything about this relationship was different. The way I was waking up each morning was different. The thoughts that passed through my head were different. It took Dave leaving me to realize that he left not because of my physical appearance, or the sex, or the way I acted. Tapping into my intuitive side, I realized that he left because energetically, we weren't on the same page. I was trying to heal him based on the expectations he wasn't measuring up to for me, but I wasn't healing myself regarding the expectations I wasn't meeting for me.

I went to my dear friend Gabriella and decided to take the first step in moving forward: learning to heal. I asked her to do an energy healing on me. We looked at some of my fears that were holding me back, and to make a long session shorter, we found that a deep fear of mine was people leaving me and not loving me for who I was. Whoa, talk about a punch to the gut. I remember leaving our session thinking about the words that came out of my own mouth, and realizing that it was the reason that for so many years I was looking for validation and affirmation in other people. I understood that was why I was struggling to love my own self, because I was scared that no one else ever would.

In those moments after my session, I finally moved forward. I recognized my inner demons, and I made the choice to face them. Now, my realization moment came to me through my energy healing session with Gabriella. Yours may come differently. It may come after a nasty breakup, or in a near-death experience, perhaps through a meditation or just a friend calling you out. It looks different for everyone, but the moment it comes is your moment to make the choice to move forward.

I went home the night of my session and started doing self-healing sessions. I chose memories from my childhood that I was holding onto for one reason or another and simply let them go. I forgave myself for harsh words I had said and actions I shouldn't have done. I chose to meditate because it made me feel good. I started journaling my thoughts and emotions that I suppressed for years on end. I dug deep inside myself and realized that displaying emotions and sharing what was on my mind was a good thing, and something I should engage in regularly. I chose to join Noom and begin my weight-loss journey, one pound at a time. I chose to have more integrity and learned to be honest, not make things up to sound good or to make others more attracted to me. Remember that list I told you to make in the beginning of this book? Slowly, day by day, I began to choose different aspects of myself to work on and to chip away at.

To this day, I am still chipping away at the things I don't love about myself, and I'm teaching myself to remove the layers that society and I have cast over my true genuineness to reveal the person I was meant to be. The best part of it all? My deepest fear that no one would love me and they would all leave disappeared. I found people who entered my life and are lifers now. Dave even came back to me for a hot second to drive this point home—that is, those who are meant to be in it for the long haul will be. I am moving forward day by day by telling myself that I want to do one or two things that make me feel good. That is the key. When it is all said and done, that love needs to come from ourselves. The whole point of moving forward and becoming heartbreak-proof is to learn to love yourself more.

It's immensely hard. To be completely transparent, it was the hardest thing I had ever done. Starting it, sustaining it. I constantly ran into obstacles, felt uncomfortable, hesitated and refused to heal some days. I cried, a lot. I fell. But I kept going. Each day that was tough, I said I was tougher. I found reasons why I was a badass. I found the good in every day. Marvel movies definitely helped a bit, but so did my meditation and workouts and food choices and psych tricks. Little by little, life got easier, and working through my inner demons wasn't as bad as I had thought. In fact, it was empowering. Each day I chose to heal a part of me, I felt myself standing up for my own beliefs, opinions, and wants. Consequently, this caused me to create boundaries and respect for myself, which ultimately led me to be heartbreak-proof. If I didn't give other people the power of love, I was giving it to myself. I for once was choosing myself and moving forward with my life as I wanted.

I still have a ways to go. Each day's a new chance to move forward. Like I said, though, life isn't all about the go, go, go. Yes, we should always be looking for ways to move our lives forward and to capitalize on new opportunities, but sometimes it is important to move back here and stay still there. That's part of living, as long as you're able to get back up on your horse and keep moving eventually.

I challenge you to break up with yourself. Maybe you're not ready yet, and that's okay! Moving forward can't be rushed, and it will happen at just the right time. But I promise you that once you embark on this phase, you will be glad you did. It can be scary and intimidating, but ultimately it is the most blissful experience of your life. You will not only begin to love yourself more but also will attract the love you desire. All you have to do is break up with yourself first, and start moving forward, because that is when you'll become heartbreak-proof.

CHAPTER 7

Rock-Bottom

It simply just wouldn't be fair of me, or right, to just leave you empty-handed after the previous chapter and tell you that you just need to go balls to the walls and complete the breakup cycle in the next couple of weeks to get yourself fully going. Heck to the no. That is the last thing I will tell you to do. In the teaching world that is what we refer to as a "burnout," and you will resent me, or even yourself, for pushing your limits and going through the motions without fully being ready for the breakup.

The truth is, the breakup cycle is long. I'm talking longgggggg. It typically is brought onto us—the most common scenario being a typical relationship. Maybe that is what resonates most with you. Maybe you just read that last chapter and decided that you are going to take the first step and get out of a tumultuous relationship tomorrow. Or maybe you are going to finally tell off your boss for being misogynistic or demeaning. Or maybe you're going to break up with your lifestyle because it's been rough the past couple of years. The breakup cycle doesn't only relate to relationships. In fact, we become heartbreak-proof when we get heartbroken in a variety of ways, whether it be a relationship, career, business venture, money—you get the idea! Whatever it is that you are breaking up with, I strongly urge you to do it if it feels right for you in whatever area of your life that is needing the breakup.

However, I know where some of you may be. Some of you may have just read that last chapter and felt completely confused, lost, or in a trance. Maybe you think that was a load of b.s. and I smoked something strong before writing that. As I have said and will continue to say, this book is based entirely on my own personal experiences, and that which I have lived through or honed in on based on my intuitive meditations.

I know the breakup cycle is confusing, daunting, and often

70

makes many of us want to run. If that is you, that's okay. I, too, ran from it for so long. I ran so flipping far that by the time I chose to finally do it, I didn't know what the devil to do or how to do it. That's why I'm writing this to you. Because I get it. I've been in your shoes. I've been the one sitting in my chair reading the latest self-help book and not understanding how the beautiful author on the front cover understands a lick of what I'm going through. I know the books and the chapters make it sound so poetic and easy, but the simple truth is, it's confusing. It's a back-and-forth battle. It's a daily struggle and quite honestly, it sucks sometimes. It's hard and tedious. But I know for myself that the breakup with myself was the most rewarding thing I could have done.

This chapter is dedicated to my rock-bottom. Like I said, I may have been so similar to you. Maybe what you read in this chapter will click, or maybe it won't. Either way, I feel that it is one of the most important parts of this book. Rock-bottom is a place that we all hit at one point in our lives or another. It looks just a tad different for each person in this world, and no two are ever the same. I know we think of rock-bottom as being the end, but I think of it as the turning point. It's the point in our lives where we choose to either stand up and fight those evil villains we've been keeping inside, or let them continue to kick the crud out of us.

Personally, I'm like Ironman, and I will choose to fight eleven times out of ten just to prove my point. But I wasn't always like that. No. Instead, for the longest time I was stuck at rock-bottom in my life: constantly pitying myself, waiting for the giving tree to bend my way just once, crying tears upon tears. In terms of the breakup cycle, I was in a constant tango with moving back and standing still. That was until 2018. Or as I like to call it, the beginning of the end of the former girl known as Hali Claire Winch.

***

December 12, 2018. This was my first day home from fall semester of my senior year at college. The previous night I had returned home, unpacked all of my belongings from school, showed off my new tattoo, and called it a night after partying a little too hard the night before. I talked with my parents a bit, I watched some Netflix, and I turned in early.

I remember waking up in a sour mood, telling myself that I was just going to work out and hopefully start to feel better. I did just that. I worked out in my old cement basement with a bike that was falling to shambles as I watched some show on TLC on a TV dated back to the prehistoric days. I went upstairs and showered in my twenty-five-year-old shower. Our bathroom was painted this wretched plum color that I begged my dad to let me use seven years prior in an attempt to "flip" my bathroom. After, I got dressed in my childhood room, the room that my parents once used, then my older brother, and finally me. I looked around at the dark grey walls that I had recently painted that July in order to change the lime green walls, to give off a more "adult" vibe to whomever would come join me for a night.

I walked out into my kitchen and looked around for food, coming up with nothing. It was around 2:00 p.m. I chose to settle on some pretzels and begin wrapping Christmas gifts. My mom had texted me around 3:00 to let me know she was going to be a little late due to a meeting, and she asked if I could turn the stove on for her. I turned the stove on, returned to my wrapping station, and continued wrapping my little heart out like the jolly Christmas elf I was.

A few minutes had passed until I noticed some smoke coming from the oven. *Great.* This literally happened all of the time. I opened the oven to notice a large grease puddle in the bottom of the rack. I began cursing out my parents who weren't even home, and eventually after three minutes of gagging over smoke and being annoyed, I wiped up the grease and threw the paper towels in the garbage. I opened the back door to air out the room, went to the bathroom, and began to feel panicked. I started shaking, and a trillion thoughts started rushing through my head, none of which I could make out.

After returning to the kitchen to realize the smoke was slowly starting to dissipate, I went upstairs to our garage apartment to check in on Granny. Granny always has a way of putting my heart at rest, and she is the first person in line to assure me that I am being absolutely ridiculous with my thoughts. I spewed out anger toward her about the grease, asked for a snack, watched a little *Ellen,* and after about five minutes, I returned back to my house feeling a little less panicked. That was until I reached the bottom of her stairs and heard the piercing sound of a fire alarm going off. My heart sank and my stomach dropped. I froze for an instant, and then began running toward the house. I flung open our front door and turned left into the dining room to realize our entire kitchen was engulfed in flames.

I ran outside, dialed 9-1-1, and got the animals outside. Next, I ran faster than lightning up Granny's stairs to get her out of her apartment, to which she questioned me with, *Well, is my apartment on fire?* Oh, how she kills me. In a matter of two minutes, my entire childhood home was engulfed in flames. My bedroom where I spent most of my time. All of my clothes, pictures, childhood memorabilia, and the last cremains of my best friend and grandfather who had passed away years before. Gone. I was the only one there to watch it, to stop it.

Much of the following hours are a blur of people, lights, and sirens. I remember watching my entire house crumble to the ground in front of me, my mom pulling me out of the road as I screamed and cried. I remember getting ushered up to a lake house by some of the most amazing people I have ever had the pleasure of knowing. There were tears, the words *I'm so sorry,* and *oh hunny, it's not your fault* being thrown everywhere. I stood in silence, astonished at what *I* had done to my family's home. This was my first rock-bottom. At the time, I thought it was my only. Oh how silly was I.

***

August 19, 2019. To save you time and energy on having to read every miniscule detail of this wretched weekend, I'll skip to the chase. Mom and I decided that after a weird year with several changes and many negatives, we were going to take off and head to Miami for a couple of days. As we headed to board the plane, the hot boy sitting across the way from me informed us that our flight was indeed canceled. I had never wanted to throat-punch someone more in my life than I did at that very moment. So, we quickly ran to the check-in point to reschedule a new flight to Miami, only to realize that the flights were all canceled and the soonest flight being scheduled to leave was for Orlando. Okay, okay. Not bad! We figured we could fly into there, book a car, and drive to Miami. LOL, what were we thinking?

Shortly after we got the car, flight, and wait time handled, we called our hotel to let them know we would be checking in real late. To our dismay, the hotel never had any reservation for us. When I tell you this day was a shit show, it was a shit show. We decided to scratch the entire thing, hopped on our flight, and flew to Orlando, where we changed our vacation destination to Clearwater instead. Upon arriving at that hotel, we realized the entire beach was flooded. You see, the "Winch Luck" was running deep that day, and my mother and I just so happened to decide we wanted to stand in the deepest current of it all. Nonetheless, we were determined to have the best vacation!

A day into our semi-decent getaway and I realized what all of the barriers we had run into on our way down to Florida were telling me. At 7:00 a.m., my mom's phone began ringing. I remember feeling groggy and confused, but I quickly panicked when I saw the name come across the caller I.D. It was my brother's girlfriend at the time. I knew at that moment that something bad had happened.

After three very frantic phone calls between my mom and the girl-friend, we learned there had been an accident with my older brother. Okay, a car accident wasn't the worst thing. It definitely could be worse, but I knew in my gut that there was more to the discombobulated story than we were getting.

Instantly, I began calling his friends, calling my friends, searching the local papers, calling my other brother and Dad. I was calling like crazy to figure out the truth to the story and what was actually happening. Apparently, we were the first to find out the news in almost real time, making us the people who were informing the locals. We called my dad, who was working on building the new house at the time. He had asked some of the workers, who informed him that there was an extremely bad accident a couple of towns over. The entire state highway was blocked. As I sit here and type this up, I still cannot conceptualize this moment in time. It stretched out over about thirty minutes, but it felt like five hours between getting the information, making calls, and checking the news. Ultimately, we heard the news that there was a car accident involving a sheriff's deputy and a civilian, with one dead and the other in critical condition.

If you can't already tell from my previous chapters, I am a bit of a bleeding heart and tend to want to fix any and all things in life to help others not have to go through pain or hardship. This is who I have been my entire life, and quite honestly I don't plan to stop anytime soon if it means I can help others. However, in this exact moment, I knew there was nothing that I could do. I knew that I could no longer control this situation, prevent the hurt, or even make the hurt go away completely. I had to swallow the pill, pull myself together, and help everyone get through it. In that exact time frame, the two victims were not identified. The families were not notified. Nothing. We had no clue if my brother was the one dead or alive, what caused the accident, or if it was even him.

About an hour and a half passed before we found out the news:

my brother had lived. Although this was a weight off of my shoulders, my heart still sank. I knew that even though I was grateful he had lived, there was someone who had died, and there will be guilt felt for that soul.

My mom and I rushed home as quickly as we could to be with my family for love and support, and we spent another couple of weeks hiding from a casualty that happened in an accident. Weeks passed, and we learned little by little what had happened and the possibilities that led to the crash. To this day it is still uncertain the exact cause, but the leading theory is carbon monoxide poisoning on my brother's behalf, which made him pass out and strike the oncoming car in the opposite lane.

It has been a year since this day, and I know my brother still feels the physical and emotional scars that the accident has left on him. My family still feels the ripple of sadness and sorrow this incident had caused. A family lost a loved one, and a person inherited guilt. It was an accident, but it doesn't make the situation any less hard. There are still news articles circulating, reports, and bad words that are spoken. I would be lying if I said it didn't hurt my heart a little more each time. When I look at my brother, my lifelong hero and first best friend, I see a guardedness. I see haunted eyes filled with survivor's guilt. I feel his anxiety.

It was from this situation, a whole year later, that I started to learn how to help others. I began to see the light in a terrible situation. I saw my purpose and my ability to heal others based on traumas. This rock-bottom, the second in an eight-month period, was one of the points at which I began to see the light in the situations I was going through. However, there were still more lessons I needed to learn.

***

October 8, 2019. Flash forward about a week prior to this date, and I was living what I thought was my best life. I was going out every weekend, getting drunk, avoiding every emotion that was coming my way, eating whatever, whenever I wanted. Oh yeah, totally living the high life. Oh, and my family was still living in our temporary living situation (a camper) due to the fire because our new house still wasn't built. Talk about yikes.

I was finishing up my master's degree and was working full-time in my first year as a teacher. I had come home one night with yet another weird feeling in my heart. My mom wasn't home, Granny's light was off in her apartment above the garage, and the ugly camper looked even uglier than normal. I walked inside where I found my dad watching Fox News alone. After about three minutes, I learned that Granny was at the hospital due to having chest pains and being unable to breathe correctly. Ugh. Now to give you a little insight, I wasn't that scared, because we were at the hospital like clockwork with Granny. In 2014, she had suffered from a TIA, which, for those who don't know, is a mini stroke. Since then, she had always had health issues. Nonetheless, she was a firecracker and rose up to beat each encounter that she had.

Granny and I share the best memories. She was my babysitter throughout my childhood, my best friend, and overall my twin in more ways than one. When one of us was irritated with someone, the other had to talk them off the ledge before we ended up in the police beat. Her laugh is more of a cackle than a belly one, her eyes sparkle blue even in her old age of seventy-four years, and her crooked walk at a snail's pace is just one of her many defining features. But boy, does she hold a special place in my heart. There have been times in my life that she easily could have beat me, kicked my ass, whatever you want to say, but hasn't. More times than not, she has gone to bat to defend my stupid ass for my latest ignorance, or covered up my tracks from my parents to avoid hearing them reprimand me as deserved.

My fondest memory is her walking into my house one weekend when I decided to throw a party when my parents left town. Music was blaring, beer was being sprayed all over, boys and girls alike were passed out all over the place. That next morning, she came down as if nothing had happened and the place wasn't a dumpster fire, she fed the animals, and walked out. She never once uttered a word to my parents, and all she said to me was *Fun night, huh?* God, that woman is a special breed.

When I had heard she was in the hospital for something to do with her breathing, I had a feeling that this would be the end. Despite my intuition, I told myself it was nothing more than the routine drill of the E.R., an overnight stay or two, and she would be perched up on her couch in her apartment in no time. I had already gone through so much in the past ten months, no way José would the universe put me through losing my best friend.

I went to the hospital the following day to talk with the doctors, where we learned this time it wasn't her typical spell. Instead, she was in heart failure, and the only way she would live would be to have a five-way bypass. Talk about someone coming up behind you to take you out by your knees. We had no idea her heart was in such bad shape. Nonetheless, we shoved positivity down her throat, told her she would be fine, and decided to transfer her to Albany Medical Center to have the surgery.

She was in that hospital for a few more days, and my family took turns driving down to see her. It was a Saturday, and I was planning to go out in Saratoga that night to see the guest star Brody Jenner at Gaffney's for much needed drinks and tomfoolery. I walked into her room and could feel her energy shift. The only way I can explain it is that I knew that she knew this was the last time I was going to be seeing her alive. We talked, and had a real talk. We talked about love, life, making memories. She told me about her furniture and what she wanted me to take, and my brothers. I brought her for a walk, and eventually found it was time to leave. She gave me her "toodle-oo" wave and turned her head toward the window as I walked out.

Three days later, as I was coming back into my classroom from teaching Social Studies, I received a call from my mom saying that Granny wasn't going to wake up from her surgery. I instantly deflated, grabbed my bag, and drove like a maniac down to Albany to bid her my final farewell. By the time I made it, I could sense her soul had already left her body.

I knew she was embarking on her new way of life, and I was empty. My best friend of twenty-three years was physically taken from the Earth, and I had officially hit another rock-bottom. I had a million thoughts running through my mind. I was thinking about her funeral, how we were going to bury her, her assets, her life, my mom. I felt the same feeling I had in the previous two rock-bottom episodes, where I knew I needed to step up and be okay in order to help, but I just didn't know how. Granny wasn't going to be alive to help me through this one.

Then, the guilt set in. I have always had the ability to talk to the other side, and fortunately I can still do that. But, my poor mom can't, or my brothers, or Granny's sister. I was the only one who could, and at that point that was the last thing I wanted to do. I didn't want to rub into everyone's faces that I can still hear her words, as could they, but they just didn't want to hone in on it. I was beyond devastated, lost, and broken. Rock-bottom hurt more than I would have ever imagined.

***

February 7, 2020. A couple of months had passed, and almost no new rock-bottom incidents had occurred in the stretch of months from Granny's passing to then. I felt like things may finally be turning around. After all, it was a new year filled with new hope and opportunities. I was ready for whatever good was going to come my way. At the time, I didn't realize I was in the standing-still phase, as well as a few slips of moving back. I was still holding onto hope of love with Dave, drinking a little too much, and constantly looking for validation and love in everyone else but myself.

Chowderfest the weekend previous had been a circus of emotions, in which I had cried my weight in tears over Dave, turned to finding love with new victims, and used food to hide all of my emotions that I was having. As a result, I ended up reaching out to an old flame in high school who I had always thought of as cute.

Enter Tanner. Tanner was a special breed. Not only was he highly attractive and the smoothest talker around, he had such a way with women that he could manipulate even the toughest to believe that he was interested in them. Oh how silly old Hali used to be.

After a few snaps and texts back and forth, the two of us decided to hang out with one another. I was stoked because he had told me he wanted to take me on a date, which is something that guys my age very rarely did anymore. To say I was on cloud nine was an understatement, especially since he was so cute. *There, this will be the way I move on from Dave and find love.* All week, I was excited to see what the date would bring, but I had a feeling that it wasn't going to go the way I had wanted it to. Nonetheless, I pushed myself to remain optimistic.

Friday night finally came around, and I heard nothing from Tanner. Nada, zilch, silence. I wasn't going to reach out, but despite my better judgement, I did. I asked him if we were still on for our date, to which he responded that since it was snowing so bad he didn't think I would want to go.

I told him I did, and we decided I would drive to his house instead to hang out. No biggie, he just wanted to hang out at his house. It was okay, it would be fine. Although I was bummed we weren't going out for a date, it was still good knowing he was interested in hanging out. I had to seize the opportunity of love while I could, after all!

Upon arrival, we began drinking, catching up, and enjoying each other's company. After too many drinks, I became too drunk to drive home and asked if I could stay, to which he informed me I could. I knew it wasn't the smartest idea, and looking back on it now I know I shouldn't have. But when drinking is involved and my self-love is low, I tend not to make the most rational of decisions for myself.

I remember saying to myself that I was safe, and Tanner wouldn't cross a line because he was friends with my brothers. But, as time passed and several attempts were made, I became less secure in my no. He continually tried to get me to say yes, but eventually I told him that wasn't my reason for coming over. To be honest, I didn't know what my reason was for coming over. Looking back now, I see it was to be validated that someone liked me enough to spend time with me, but self-love-deprived Hali didn't see that.

One hour passed, then two, and then three. I stopped drinking because I wanted to go home, but I needed to sober up. I didn't call for a ride because I didn't want Tanner to think negatively of me, but I should have. Each time I said no, he cared less and less, until eventually he didn't care at all. His need and want to have sex overpowered my ability to resist, and Tanner ended up taking advantage of me in the situation. Not all of what happened was his fault, as I did put myself in that situation. However, his lack of respect and crude manner with which he used me set me over the edge of self-hatred. I laid in his bed after the act of unwanted sex and cried. I cried because I didn't and couldn't fight back. I cried because I was ashamed. I cried because he told me it was our secret. I cried because I had such little respect for myself that I put myself in the situation to begin with.

I would be doing you a disservice to not include this crucial rock-bottom moment in my life. It was beyond hard to write this section, and took a lot of convincing from loved ones and my counselor to include it, but I ultimately hope this is one that can make an impact on your life. If not yours, someone else who may have been part of something like this. It was at the point of Tanner taking advantage of me that I realized I was at my absolute rock-bottom. I hated myself every day for what happened, and I was so embarrassed and ashamed that it was my fault that I refused to tell my family. My brothers were friends with Tanner, for God's sake! However, with time and the right people, I felt comfortable enough to share my story, and ultimately, the lesson it taught me. If it wasn't for Tanner, I wouldn't know how to become heartbreak-proof, and wouldn't be able to help you do the same. This was the point in my life that I decided to make the change.

The years spanning from 2018–2020 were less than kind to my family and me. The amount of times that we ended up in the news that year was beyond the number of times that I would have ever wanted to be. In all the bad that rock-bottom had to offer, though, I learned through several months, countless meditations, and therapy that everything that happened had a purpose. Now, I'm not going to get on my soapbox and preach that everything in life happens for a reason. No. Heck to the flipping no. But what I will say is that through every crisis that was faced, there was a greater reason for why it happened. I learned lessons that made me look deeper within myself in order to heal. I had to learn how to count on myself, my love for who I was, to pull myself out of a depression, out of an anxiety attack, out of a fog, in order to keep pushing every day to obtain the life I want most.

I lost everything in these few years. Between the fire, the accident, the loss of Granny, and Tanner, I lost what I had deemed as my life. I lost every blessed item that I had collected from childhood. I lost pictures, trinkets, toys, clothes, money (so much cash), my baby blanket. I lost memorabilia that I would never be able to replace again in my life. I lost the "home" that I thought was going to be there my entire life. But, I gained a new understanding and gratitude for people. I have a newfound respect for putting down my phone, not snapping a picture of an event or situation, and instead reveling in the moment. I learned that things don't hold a memory, but emotions related to the memory do. Songs, people, places, conversations. I learned that items can be replaced, but people cannot. Nor can the time that you spend with people be replaced. I began to realize that people who surrounded me my entire life, who I had overlooked, were family. I began to see more of the meaning of life. I saw that a helping hand, a tight hug, and the simple words "I love you" were more important than any materialistic thing I could ever own.

I began to see life from a whole new perspective. Families and community members and associations were donating food, money, services, and love to my family through each tragedy, just out of the kindness of their own hearts. We didn't ask, and they didn't need us to. I began noticing how people can show unconditional love without being prompted, just because they had enough to spare. I would never wish the experiences that I went through on anyone else in this world, but I am grateful that I went through them. For each situation, I was given the opportunity to look at the situation as a whole, rather than a single instant. Initially, when the fire happened, I remember thinking, *This is the worst thing that could happen.* I had a narrow perspective. I pitied myself and my family for having to go through such a horrific accident, and I felt as though the sympathy and food was needed. But as the year progressed and other less-significant tragedies (such as my dad cutting his thumb off with a table saw on Easter morning) began to occur, I had the opportunity to look at my life from an outsider's perspective.

I was in Chicago in mid-July for a nannying gig, having an amazing weekend away from New York. Finally, I started to feel like I was getting out of the funk that I was in and was meeting and spending time with some incredible people. My anxiety and depressed attitude were slowly dissipating, and that nightmare life finally felt as though it was slowly melting away. That was until I had gotten a frantic call from Mom about a suicide attempt that had occurred at home with a family member. For personal reasons,

I won't get into the specifics, but I remember getting the call and feeling absolutely hopeless. I could feel my anxiety rising, and my control slipping away. I began sobbing in my hotel room all alone, feeling sorry for myself that I wasn't with my family, and thinking that this was yet another terrible thing that was happening to us. After about a ten-minute panic attack, I decided to take a shower and go out on my balcony overlooking the beautiful sights of downtown Chicago.

In that moment, I began to realize that I was seeing the situation from a narrow lens. Yes, the fire sucked, and the other incidents that had occurred recently were less than favorable. However, there was still light to be seen. I still had most of my family. In fact, my brothers and I had gotten closer throughout the year due to the circumstances. I was helping to make my mom happier on a daily basis just by being home more, and I was helping my Dad around the house when I could to make jobs easier. I was talking to my extended family more and letting my guard down. I was hugging other people, saying "I love you" more, and actually enjoying each day as it came because I didn't know if it would be my last. I was in Chicago, one of the most beautiful cities in the world, looking over the Riverwalk on my own agenda, with everything being paid for. I guess in that ten-minute span that I spent looking down from my balcony, I began to realize the biggest lesson that applied to my life and the events that had yet to unfold that year: there is always something that you can love in your life.

As the year went on and the traumas continued to pile up, I kept reminding myself of this. After my brother's accident, I reminded myself that this was a lesson to be safer, more appreciative, more positive. I love my brother more than life itself, but I didn't do my best to make it known. I put up the highest guard against my heart, and always felt that if I was telling people that I loved them then I was acting soft. I realized that life was meant to be filled with love, whether we're giving it to other people or ourselves.

After Granny passed away, I yet again learned that I wasn't giving validation to others about how much I loved them. I realized that there were always more times and situations where I could spend more quality time with others. There were more opportunities right in front of me that I could have taken advantage of to make more memories. Tanner taught me that I needed to love myself instead of looking for it in others, because sometimes it can be taken to an extreme. I learned that if I wanted to stop being taken advantage of, I needed to assert my wants and needs with myself above others. Loving myself wasn't selfish, it was necessary.

Yes, those couple of years sucked a big one. There is no way I will deny that. However, once I stopped pitying myself and the situations I was in, I began to take on a new appreciation of life. Up until 2020, I had spent the vast majority of my life refuting my abilities or downplaying my life for the sake of others instead of enjoying each moment that was presented to me. I chose to take a negative outlook on situations in order to fit in with others or to make myself feel worse about whatever it was that I was facing. I chose to stand still in life while everything was happening instead of taking life by the hand and making the most of the moments that unfolded. The biggest change I made, though, was the choice to start loving. I began loving others, and making it known that I loved them. I wouldn't leave my friends or my parents without telling them I loved them. I began using love as an adjective to describe my feelings and passions. Best of all, I dug deep inside of myself to figure out what it was that I loved doing and what made me feel good.

With all of the bad that happened and the anxiety and depression I was experiencing, I decided that night in Chicago that I needed to learn to let it go. I had to make the conscious choice to let situations go that were out of my control, while also dealing with the emotions that were associated with them. As I did this, I began to learn how to love at the same time. For example, when my brother's accident happened, I felt guilty, sad, scared, angry. I felt an array of emotions, but instead of pushing down those emotions, I sat with them in meditation. I would sit and think of the emotions I was feeling, and I asked myself how I could turn them into love. I thought about the guilt I felt for my brother and the situation that I couldn't change for him, and decided that sending him love was something I could do. I recognized I was sad that he had to go through something so horrific, but I loved that he was getting his own help to work through it. I was scared that there would be lawsuits and hate and legality issues, but I loved that I would be standing right by his side through the situation to offer support. No matter what the emotion was that I was feeling, I fought it back harder with love. Eventually, the negative emotions began to evaporate, and love started to fill the voids. This not only made me feel better, but it started to show my brother that some light could be shed on such a horrific accident.

I then turned to the things I loved most: teaching, being social, doing readings, helping others. I chose to start doing something I loved at least once a day. I was meditating each night before bed, journaling, teaching during the day, doing readings on the weekend, and helping my parents around the house. I started to do things that made my heart happy. I chose to put myself in situations and surround myself by those who made me feel good. I started to take back control over my life in order to love every day that was thrown my way.

Now, by no means did this happen overnight. In fact, it took almost a year to fully grasp the concept that I had control over how my life played out. I could have taken (and sometimes did) my circumstances as they came, done nothing about them, and pitied myself for the crap I was going through. That would have been very easy. Everyone was already feeling sorry for me, so I could have easily complied with their sorrows and done nothing with my emotions until my anxiety and depression took over and I was living a life I hated. I did do that sometimes. There were some nights

I couldn't get out of bed because I would get so wrapped up in my own anxiety that I couldn't fathom going to hang out with friends who hadn't lived through the same crises I had gone through. There were points where I would want to throat-punch my brothers who would return to their apartments and not spend time with my parents, and I felt responsible for making sure they were okay. I had several times where I was down in my feels and felt alone. That is normal, and that is okay.

The most important part of the journey was when I learned that I didn't have to feel that way all the time. I learned that it was okay to be happy, and to want to be happy for myself. I learned that loving myself and my life was my choice, and no one else had a say in it. I learned how to assert myself and to speak up when it was most needed so others didn't control my life. I learned to take control over my life to become heartbreak-proof. Yes, life had given me many lemons those years, but the important part was turning those lemons into lemonade. And that was exactly what I did. When the tragedies finally halted for a couple of months, I chose to take control over my life. I reflected on what I wasn't loving about myself or my life, and chose one thing that I wanted to change.

My biggest thing—my weight. I was a compulsive binge-eater as a result of the year I had, and I became grotesquely overweight and unhealthy. In March of 2020, I finally got up enough strength to join Noom and take one step in the right direction of changing my life.

As I said, my mind-shift and change of lifestyle didn't happen overnight. There were weeks where I chose to make myself feel better, only for the next week to feel like garbage again. Our journeys to self-love and becoming heartbreak-proof by taking control over our lives aren't smooth or easy. In most cases, it's hard as fudge and in a zigzag pattern. The important part, though, is that we make the choice to change it. I could have easily stayed at rock-bottom. I could have invited more pity into my life, followed by sorrow, anxiety and depression. I could have rolled in free meals and handouts that entire time, but it didn't sit right with me.

I didn't like being at rock-bottom. I didn't like the constant negative feeling I would have when I woke up in the morning, or the utter self-hatred I felt when I looked at myself in the mirror or when I snapped at a loved one. So instead, I chose to fill my life with love. And let me tell you, once I did this, the love didn't stop coming!

The purpose of this chapter is not to make you feel sorry for me. Trust me, I had enough of that. Instead, I want you to see how you can apply a similar mentality to your life. Perhaps you have already hit rock-bottom, and you've been struggling to get back afloat after it. Maybe you've been having a hard time getting to the point in your life when you're finally happy and love each day you're given. Or perhaps you haven't even hit rock-bottom yet, but you've been in similar situations or have had this feeling of negativity surround you for so long that you want to break it!

Think about a situation or experience that you've had where it took the wind out of you; one where you didn't think you would be able to come back from. What types of emotions were you feeling when you experienced it? Sit with those emotions for a minute or two, and recall as many as you can.

Once you've recalled the emotions, write them down on a piece of paper or in your phone so you can visibly see them. After you write them down, think of how you can respond to them with love. Can you send your soul love? Can you forgive yourself? Can you think of the good that came out of the situation? Or perhaps you can think of someone who made you feel loved in the situation. Bringing love to the situation helps to squash the feelings and emotions that are holding you back and bringing you down, and gives you the ability to move past it to better days. Love is the opposite of negativity, and it helps to kill the negative fire. The more love you can bring to your own personal situation, the more uplifted and empowered you will feel when you think of it!

Now that you are feeling a little brighter and more positive, even if it is the slightest amount, go do something right now that will bring you happiness and that you will love. Maybe it's giving a hug to a loved one, petting your dog, or going for a run. Whatever the action is, go do it. Trust me, it will make you feel better. Once we hit rock-bottom, or really any type of bottom that is associated with negativity, we have to hit it back with love. The more love we pour into the situation, the better chance we have at becoming resilient and overcoming it. Not to mention, you're showing yourself love by not harboring negative emotions that will weigh you down. Becoming heartbreak-proof comes when you have so much love for yourself that even the most negative of situations can't break you. You fight back with love so hard that it's all you feel.

So what are you waiting for? Drag your behind out of rock-bottom and start on your road to love! Go! I promise it will be the best choice you've made in a while, and you'll be that much closer to becoming heartbreak-proof.

CHAPTER 8

Meditation and Intuition

Ah, my dear friend. Once my foe, the one that was pushed back against, the one thing in this world that would make swallowing glass look more enjoyable. *Screw meditation,* as I used to say. Oh, how the tables have turned.

The purpose of including a chapter on this "hippy" or "zen" crap is because of the true value of it. I, like maybe some of you, pushed meditation out of my life for the longest time. I grew up in a family where the word *meditation* was hardly spoken, much less practiced. I thought for the longest time that meditation was simply an act that only monks in the mountains of Iceland practiced.

Here's the thing with meditation—it's an overlooked necessity to life. Yup, you heard me. And as you have probably guessed, meditation only helps to evolve your sense of self-love, which inadvertently makes you heartbreak-proof. So, cheers to meditation!

Like I said, I grew up not knowing the first thing about meditation. In my psychology class during my Freshman year of college, my professor announced to the class at midterm time that we were all going to devote ten minutes of class to self-meditation. She shut off the lights, played music that sounded like someone peeing on the floor, and sat cross-legged on the front table. The first thought that popped into my mind was, *This lady has absolutely lost her marbles.* Followed by, *I'm going to have a panic attack,* then on to my personal favorite, *Eff this.* Needless to say, I wasn't feeling the whole zen-and-relaxed vibe that day. Not to mention, I was in a class of thirty-five strangers, some of them hot boys, and others were girls who were not buying the whole thing, either. I certainly did not have enough confidence in that moment to let go of my own ego and try meditating. On the other hand, I had no clue HOW to meditate.

My professor started by asking us to close our eyes and to sit comfortably in our chair. She began breathing deep into her belly and out her mouth, and then told us all to focus on our breath. Ha. That has been the one thing I have never been able to do my entire life. In fact, when people would tell me to focus on my breath when I was younger, it would induce a full-blown anxiety attack. I didn't know how to "breathe into my belly" or "focus on my lungs filling with oxygen." So, instead of asking questions and trying, I simply sat in my chair, mortified, as I watched all of the "cool" kids laughing at my professor. If you couldn't tell, I was really into giving others and myself labels during this time. At the end of that class, I packed up as quickly as I could and ran out to the car. Thank Jesus I had escaped that one.

Although I thought I was in the clear, it was as if that one time in psych class opened the floodgates to the world of meditation for me. I was being presented with opportunities in fitness classes, recreational activities, even at work, to embrace meditation and try connecting with my inner self. *What the actual frick?* If you're anything like me in my earlier years, you may have run into similar thoughts such as this. Meditation was extremely foreign to me, so embracing it and practicing it was like accepting the plague to be a part of my immune system. Ain't gonna happen, boss! Over the years to come, I refused meditation more and more, at every opportunity I could. At this point in my life, I was experiencing a boatload of anxiety, some depression, and overall an ugly perception of who I was. I hated being alone and allowing my thoughts to run rapidly through my head, so at some level, I knew that if I meditated I would be facing my worst nightmares head-on. And let's face it, none of us want to do that. That was until I had no other choice.

When I met Gab at college and learned she was a medium, I thought that was the definition of "cool." I couldn't stop thinking about how amazing it would be to connect with dead people, talk with those that I've lost, and help others connect to their loved ones. I was always perplexed with how people did it, and how they were just born with the sense of connecting to the other side, so I began asking questions. I wanted to know more and more about her abilities, and eventually, we became great friends and bonded through my inquiries.

When she told me I had the innate ability to do the same thing, I just about passed out. How could I, Hali Winch, the girl from a small town that no one knows about in New York, have the ability to help people connect with spirit? No way. I wasn't born with the gift, nor had I ever connected with anyone to deliver messages to other people. Sure, I had connected with my great-grandfather, and Grampy, and my friend, Jake, who had all passed, but that wasn't talking to the dead. That was just my inner thoughts that came to me, or my crazy-ass dreams I was having at night because I ate too much ice cream before bed. Clearly, Gab had no clue what she was talking about!

Oh, but she did. Little did I know that this "meditation" gig was the way through which I could connect with spirit in a more controlled manner. The reason why I hadn't been experiencing spirit beforehand was because of my straight refusal to engage in the act of connecting with my inner self. Hence, this was why spirit was coming to me in my "thoughts" (really my inner self projecting itself into my conscious thoughts) and my dreams (my subconscious making its appearance to my conscious). Holy yikes.

I knew when I figured out that I, in fact, possessed the innate ability to connect with spirit, that I couldn't turn a blind eye. My whole purpose in life has always been to help people by making them love themselves. I had seen how mediums all around the world have been able to bring peace, closure, and happiness to those longing for another conversation with their loved ones, which ultimately led them to living a better, more fulfilled life.

So, I chose to suck up my own fear and connect with my inner self through meditation. Gulp. Jesus, was I scared. I didn't know what to expect. Would all of my darkest, worst inner thoughts come to mind? Would I see thoughts and emotions that I had been suppressing for years come to the surface? Would I even be able to connect with spirit in a way that helps other people? Everything was so unknown, so confusing and scary. That's right, I was scared of meditation. The one thing on this Earth that is supposed to bring us peace, a sense of grounding, and a way of awakening to our highest selves. Yup, I wanted to run. But I didn't.

Gab took me through my first meditation. She played the "zen" music, put on her oil diffuser, turned on her faux waterfall, and away we went. We sat in silence for about ten minutes, and she turned the music off and asked how I felt. I told her, "Great," which she clearly knew was a lie.

So, I admitted to her that I had no clue how to friggin' meditate. What was I supposed to think about, or not think about? How did I connect with my breath? How was this meditation supposed to help me talk to dead people? All I kept hearing was the music, and all I was seeing was different thoughts that came to my mind—the beach, waterfalls, guys I liked, etc. I was defeated. I thought to myself, *This is supposed to be easy. Everyone can meditate. Why can't I? Maybe I'm not cut out for this after all.*

Gab could see the defeat written all over my face. She encouraged me to keep trying, but next time, forget what I think I know and just go with the unknown.

I didn't know what on God's green earth that meant. To be honest, no one knows what the unknown is, other than that it's indeed unknown. That night, I went back to my house, sat on my bed, and meditated. I again saw different pictures, some colors, heard the music playing in the background, but I didn't get in touch with any spirits. I didn't hear any messages. I didn't see a different version of myself or hear those inner thoughts that I had been hiding for so long. I just sat in confusion with an overabundant amount of thoughts about how I wasn't doing it right.

I continued to push myself to meditate: sitting with music in the background, trying to force all of my thoughts and images away. I tried each day with no success, until finally I just wanted to give up. Gab had invited me to sit in on a reading for a friend of hers, to which I agreed. I knew I would unfortunately have to meditate (a.k.a., sit and pretend I know what I'm doing). I told myself that after that reading, I would decide if I wanted to continue on the journey of meditating.

Once more, I sat in a room with an oil diffuser, faux waterfall, "zen" music, and this time a salt lamp and crystals. I closed my eyes to try to hear messages that may have been for the young lad coming in for the reading, but nothing. Zilch. Nada. I was over it. About ten minutes after the meditation, her friend arrived, and we began the reading.

Gab did the reading, and I was amazed. She was pulling information through for this kid that no one could have possibly known. I was astounded by the messages she heard and her ability to communicate with him on a soul level. I was sitting and watching the entire reading as if it was an episode of my favorite TV show.

That was until she turned the reading over to me. *Hali, what did you hear?* No. No. No. Absolutely not. I couldn't hear diddly squat during my meditation, and she wanted *me* to give this boy his reading? No. Not happening.

I cleared my throat and stared at this boy for what felt like two hours. Finally, I began to speak. But instead of pulling from what I had seen during my meditation, I started to spew words out of my mouth that I had never heard. They were so foreign to me, but they resonated so much with the boy. After about ten minutes, I stopped and looked at him.

He had tears in his eyes and validated each message that I had given him. He was beyond thankful for what I had said, and I had very little recollection of what I had said. When it was all done, he thanked us and left.

I turned to Gab and asked her how in the world I was able to pull those messages through, doubting that I even did, and she told me: *By connecting with your inner self.* What? How? I literally just sat and listened to the music! How did I connect to anything? And that's when it clicked with me.

Meditation isn't meant to look the same way for any two people. In fact, meditation is a different experience for everyone who does it. Spiritual people aren't the only ones who benefit from it. Meditation isn't a way that connects you with spirit. It isn't only meant to connect you with your breath. Your mind doesn't have to go blank or focus intently on one thing. Meditation is simply the act of connecting with yourself in whatever way feels right to you!

After that encounter with my first reading, I stopped focusing on how to connect with spirit through meditation, and I focused more on connecting with myself. I started first by sitting in a silent room, closing my eyes, and taking three deep breaths. I didn't focus on where the breaths were going, and I didn't attempt to see a specific picture or hear a specific mantra in my head. I just sat in silence and listened to my own thoughts.

When I first began, I heard a lot about what happened on a given day (mostly because I meditated right before bed). I would see different scenarios that occurred throughout the day, along with the emotions that were evoked because of the situations. As I became more practiced, I began diving into my emotions that I was feeling, and figuring out the thoughts or memories that were connected to those emotions.

Through healing sessions, my own meditation, and readings from other spiritual coaches and professionals, I started to learn how to focus my meditation on specific moments in time, unresolved issues, and even the future. I learned that through meditation, I could destress by working with my mind and body to let go of unnecessary tension that is no longer serving me. I was taught how to connect with angels and spirit guides and, yes, spirit in general. I learned how to connect to other worlds and times, and how to manifest my own life. Recently I have learned how to control my thinking and tap into my highest self in order to control my current reality. I learned how to live the life that I have been destined to lead based on what I heard my own thoughts saying in meditation. I have finally learned to connect with myself in order to live out my life's purpose, all because I gave meditation a shot in the dark (quite literally).

You may be sitting in the same position that I sat in years ago. Meditation may seem so extremely foreign to you, or unnecessary. Maybe you don't even feel compelled to do it. That is okay. I never want to force you into thinking a certain way or doing as I do, but instead, I'm just telling you from experience what has helped me tap into my inner self to love who I am unconditionally. Meditation was scary for me. I didn't want to have to relive specific memories in time or feel unwanted emotions that I worked for so long to let go of. I was worried that meditation would only increase my anxiety and drive me to a dark world that I couldn't come back from. I thought that if people found out I was meditating, they would label me as "weird" or call me a hippy.

The day I stopped letting my ego control my thoughts of the world around me and subconsciously constructing my own reality was the same day I gave meditation a try and I began to love myself. Meditation connected me with my intuition, or my sense of self. I was able to have a better grasp of the emotions I was feeling, what was causing them, and I was learning that it was okay to feel them. It helped me to learn that I had the ultimate say in how I feel, when I feel, and why I feel what I do in any given situation.

The best part of meditation? It's a free way to become heart-break-proof. It can happen anywhere you want. There have been times where I am exhausted mentally and physically from work or life, and I sit in my car for two minutes and just breathe. I give myself a few minutes to feel my emotions and hear my thoughts, acknowledge them, and start moving forward again.

Guess what? THAT'S NORMAL. We are in a world that looks at those who process their emotions outwardly as being "too much" or "too weird" or "too liberal" or "too fantasy." You want to know what I say? That's too many unnecessary labels.

You wanna know what else I say? We need to feel these emotions within ourselves in order to make ourselves heartbreak-proof. The more we suppress our emotions, the greater the chance we will carry them forward into new relationships and scenarios in life that cause us to get heartbroken. Ever heard the expression, *Doing the same thing over and over again, but expecting different results?* Albert Einstein coined this as the definition of insanity, but I call it heartbreak. We can't push away our feelings and wounds and expect a different outcome each time. In order to become heartbreak-proof, you have to heal what is broken. The best way to do that? Meditating and listening to yourself. What does your soul need? What do you need?

Again, I am not telling you to go lock yourself in your room for ten minutes with that "zen" music playing, close your eyes, and meditate. I strongly suggest it (especially for those of you who have kids or a significant other or a job or a busy life), but I would never force you to do it. It can be scary. Meditating allows your mind to disconnect with the world around you, the world we know and are comfortable with, and instead, it allows you to connect you with your inner world. From the time we are young, we are instantly disconnected from this inner world. We are shown by our parents, teachers, community, and society that we don't have a say in several matters. Our voices don't count when we are kids, because we don't know as much as adults do. That inner voice in your head? That's just your imagination talking to you. And this couldn't be the furthest thing from the truth. That voice inside your head is your intuition, your inner self. And he/she is dying to connect with you in order to help you live your best life.

That's right, not only mediums like me or spiritual influencers like Gab have intuition. We are all innately born with our own sense of intuition. It comes in the form of inner voices, inner dialogues, gut feelings, passions, etc. We all have intuition, but so few of us know how to foster it in order to make something of it. Our intuition is our soul's purpose of being here on this Earth, and it's about time we harness it in order to make that beautiful person inside of you shine out and light up our world. How do we do that exactly? Meditation is definitely the best way, in my opinion. But if that's not your thing, listen to yourself!

When you meet someone and don't get the best feeling when you shake their hand, listen to yourself. That is your intuition's way of telling you they probably don't belong in your life. When you don't feel like you should go to a certain event, party, work function, etc., listen to yourself. That is your intuition's way of telling you that isn't in alignment with you, or something may happen that you shouldn't be a part of. When you get the butterflies in your stomach and you want to jump up and down while shouting hooray, listen to yourself. Your intuition is telling you you're aligning with your purpose, and you are meant to embark on that journey. Whatever the scenario is, listen to what your body is telling you. Hear the thoughts that go through your head, and feel the emotions that pulsate through your blood. Be present with yourself.

I promise once you start doing this, you'll never want to stop. Meditating and connecting with your own intuition helps you not only live your best life possible, but it makes you fall in love with life in general. You stop giving other people the control to run your life, and instead you take back the reins in order to call the shots. You find yourself in situations that are aligned with your purpose, desires, and passions. You see that you start surrounding yourself with people who help you grow and make you feel good. When this all starts to happen, you become heartbreak-proof, because you are where your life is meant to be!

All you have to do is start listening to yourself, your inner self.

Personally, I did that through meditation and being mindful. Everyone can do it; it's just a matter of trying. You may not enjoy it the first round (or twenty, if you're me), but eventually you'll start to look forward to sitting or lying in your bed with soft music playing in the background, breathing deeply and processing your thoughts and emotions.

Connecting with your inner self is blissful and empowering, so I challenge you to do it. Give it a try! Who knows, maybe you'll be the next person who can change this world! All you have to do is listen and trust yourself. Only then will you learn to love who you are from the inside out, which will help make you heartbreak-proof.

CHAPTER 9

Self-Discovery

Once I started to train my intuition, I started to learn how to love myself, which ultimately led me to becoming heartbreak-proof. I began taking a deeper look inside of who I was, what I wanted, and what I was capable of.

Remember how I said meditation will bring you through those fears and feelings you've kept suppressed for so long? Yup. It happened to me. I'm talking feelings, thoughts, truths, and stories that I had kept stuffed down for years were finally coming to the light. This was one of the hardest things I had to do. I was scared, nervous; lord, I was having full-blown anxiety attacks. I would begin a meditation, start to hear something that scared me or that I didn't want to deal with, and would quickly come back to consciousness in order to avoid feeling my feelings or facing truths that I didn't want to.

You wanna know what happened every time I did that? You guessed it. I was staying still and allowing my heart to be broken from the same wounds because I refused to heal and learn the lessons. I wasn't moving forward, I wasn't loving myself any more than I had the day before, and I definitely wasn't attracting the love that I wanted for my whole life.

Finally, in February of 2020, I decided I was done hiding. After the disastrous years I had been through prior, I knew I had gone through it all for a reason. I had two choices—I could continue to stand still and be heartbroken by my current reality, or choose to move forward and refuse to let others break my heart anymore. That day in February was the first day of my self-discovery, and it hasn't stopped since.

Let me expose myself real quick. From the time I was little, I always remember telling white lies (or not so white) on the reg. I would tell lies to make myself sound cooler, more fun, more likeable, or even to get out of sticky situations (you know, the kind where you hurt your brother but you don't want to get in trouble with your mom). However, I found that with each lie I told, I got myself further and further from the truth.

I think the first lie I told was when I was about four. My parents had asked why I was up so early, and why I was upstairs in their room when my room was downstairs. Well Tess and John, my grubby little hands were searching through your closet because I knew there were toys hidden in the back, so I was sneaking up there to grab my new Barbie. But instead of saying that, I told them I was just seeing if they were up. I had ripped open the Barbie in the closet and ended up playing with it for twenty minutes after I was caught. Although this was a minor infraction on my behalf, it was the first of many.

I didn't lie often to my parents when I was younger, unless I was trying to get out of trouble. No, instead the lying mostly took place with my "friends." When I was in elementary and middle school, there weren't the best of people to hang with. I was always so different than everyone else. Many of the girls didn't enjoy me because I was annoying or differed in beliefs from them, and the boys were into farming, which was the furthest thing from my interest.

I grew up in a family that was primarily centered around baseball and travel, and I had different experiences of traveling around the East Coast with friends who became family. My friends in elementary school rarely left our town, let alone the state, and came from families that were run by grandparents or single mothers or aunts. I think part of the reason I was so estranged from them was because I couldn't relate. I didn't know how to talk to people who had so much hate, negativity, and bitterness from traumatic childhoods when my was the furthest from it. I became the oddball out with my overexcited joy for everyday life, my stories of different baseball players I had the pleasure of meeting, and the love I carried for those in my life.

So, I lied to make them like me. I would tell lies about farms I had visited with my parents, vacations we went on and excursions that we did. I would make fun of myself and tell stories about funny things I did just to make everyone around me laugh. Again, simple stuff, nothing too major.

For the majority of my teenage years, this is exactly how it went. I was constantly on this hamster wheel of lies or exaggerations in order to sound cooler, funnier, smarter, or more experienced. I moved to a new school in tenth grade, and I told myself that once I moved to this new school with new people that I would stop the lying. I would share my actual opinions on matters or show my sweet side that coincided with my funny. I would be genuine with others and show that I can be fun while also being serious. I would show that yes, my brothers were extremely athletic, but so was I, and I was smart and well-rounded, just like I always thought they were. I was off to a good start, mentally. I was ready to tackle my new school with new people, and to debut my real self for once in my entire life.

That mentality lasted until the school year started. You see, I was on the field hockey team, and it was easy to be myself. There really wasn't much time to make up stories or crack ridiculous jokes. We ran, did drills, ran some more, and then practice was over. Simple. The hard part came when I went to actual high school. There were boys, cliques, new teachers, and a new place in the world where I didn't quite fit in. I hung around my field hockey girls, but I felt like the outcast since I was new and no one knew who I was. I began fake-laughing at people's jokes, because everyone else did. I would make fun of others who I personally had no problem with, and then I eventually started making up stories and lies about the reasons I had moved to my new school.

I can remember starting field hockey on my new team in tenth grade. I was surrounded by older girls who were extremely popular and fit the exact description of being "it" girls. They possessed every possible characteristic that I fell short of, so naturally I chose to match them in order to be accepted. I attempted (and failed) to be flirty, calm, cool, nondramatic, athletic, etc. I told them I had left my old school due to them not having a great field hockey program and because I was bullied by other girls. This was half true, but I never disclosed that their field hockey program was my last priority when I was there, or the fact that I was one of the biggest bullies to others prior to getting called a lesbian by the same group of girls I once stood proudly with. Although it was half true, it was still a lie because it's not completely true. Only, my fourteen-year-old self didn't see it that way.

Quickly, I fell back into the patterns I was convinced I was going to be able to break. Again, these stories and exaggerations were nothing major, but they were far enough from the truth that they hid who I was. I was so desperate to fit in with everyone else and be "normal" that I lost sight of who I was or why I was special. I fell into relationships, friendships, and habits that didn't suit me. As a result, I was unhappy and was getting my heart broken on the reg by myself.

Don't get me wrong, I had a wonderful high-school experience and made awesome friendships and relationships, but I wasn't being the most genuine I could be. I wasn't truly fulfilled and happy, and as a result, I found myself falling out of touch with friends or getting my heart broken by guys. I was giving them the power to love me instead of loving myself.

This continued into my early adulthood, until I started at my four-year college. I can remember starting at Saint Rose and thinking that my life was going to again remain the same. No boyfriend, barely any genuine friends, the same habits, the same insecurities. You get the picture. In my third week of being at the college, I was given the opportunity to join the school's cheerleading team. I had been a cheerleader my whole life and absolutely loved the sport.

However, I was a far cry from the peppy, enthusiastic, stunt-flying, acrobatic tumbler that you see on most teams in high school. You see, in my high school it was more of a joke, and god forbid people would look at me in a negative way. Despite my negative self-talk and lack of self-confidence, I tried out for cheer. To my surprise, I made the team.

Once I made the team, I began getting close with two girls who really made some of the largest impacts on my life. Jordan and Grace were constantly spreading kindness, positivity, and really are the reason I was able to break my awful habit of lying. Over the course of the seasons I was at Saint Rose, the three of us became friends and would hang out in each other's dorms, on the weekends, and would even do hometown trips together. Once I became friends with them, I realized that my lies weren't needed. I didn't have to inflate the amount of boyfriends I have had or change my viewpoint on life to make it a negative one. Instead, I was able to talk freely, be emotional when I needed to be, tell a good joke and have a good laugh. Our friendship came naturally, and for the first time in the longest time, I didn't feel like I had to make up lies in order for them to want to be around me.

I am truly grateful for their friendship and their ability to make it so easy to be myself, but it didn't help me to generalize that feeling to others in my life. The truth of the matter was, I had other friends who weren't as easy to get along with and were more judgmental, so the facade had to continue. The "fake" Hails was spinning a tale and making up stories left and right for laughs and good times. On occasion, these friends would ask to hear one of the stories I had made up again, but I would fail to because I couldn't even remember what it was that I told them in the first place. I would laugh it off and pretend I knew the gist of the story but end up falling short with an "oh, ya know the rest!" I was desperate for them to continue seeing me in the best, funniest light possible. But in February of 2020, my meditation brought forth what was really going on; I was hanging onto these friendships because I thought they liked me, and I was petrified to get my heart broken once more. I was choosing to hang around Negative Nellies and Suppressed Sallies because they would laugh at my jokes or think of me as a "god" for my sense of humor and the life that I have "lived."

My friends I met during college didn't view me in this way. Of course they thought I was funny, but they didn't put me in a different category from themselves. I wasn't better or worse, or needed more or less care. I wasn't someone who didn't have emotions or had an easier/harder life, nor were my stories any funnier than their own. They didn't like me, either. They loved me. They took me in and treated me like family. They would lay down the cold hard truth more often than not, and call me on my b.s. They were transparent with me.

After my meditation, I chose to take a hard look at my life and my relationships with coworkers, family, friends, and potential mates. I chose to meditate on each one, and really look at the feeling I would get associated with each one. Did my stomach go in knots when I thought about hanging out with them, or would I get butterflies of excitement because I never knew what was going to come next? Did I feel anxious because they might ask me about a story that I made up to impress them, or did I feel safe and compelled to talk about my feelings with them? My intuition guided me, and I found that more often than I cared to admit, some of the people I spent my time with gave me that icky feeling in my stomach. I didn't like hanging out with many of these people, but instead I liked that they laughed with me or pretended to like me.

After further meditation and following my intuition, I discovered that the reason I was lying all along was to prevent people like that from walking out of my life and leaving me heartbroken. I hated being the reject, the girl who no one wanted at their house or at their sleepover. I despised being the girl that was left out from a GNO or a dinner night, or the topic of conversation. I was scared.

I was self-conscious. I didn't love myself enough to know that the people who are meant to be in my life won't leave me, no matter what. I chose to fake it 'til I make it, rather than take my mask off and let the world see who I was. I didn't know how to become heartbreak-proof, so these people didn't do the heartbreaking for me.

That meditation was a turning point for me. I started to look at what my world around me looked like, and found that I was hiding so much of myself behind a mask of lies, which ultimately brought in the wrong kind of love from others. I was reflective on the relationships I was in. I even looked at my career and found that I was pushing down my positive nature, genuine happiness, strong-willed opinion, and desire to do right by the students in order to have my coworkers like me. This was scary. I was seeing the world that I had lived in for so long come crumbling down around me. I wasn't who I thought I was, nor was I the person who so many people thought I was. These thoughts about genuineness came crashing into me from my subconscious mind, where I suppressed them for so many years. They needed to be heard and to be let free. So, that's exactly what I did.

I stopped. I took a break. I didn't use social media. I stopped texting people back. I stopped exaggerating and making up stories for people who didn't matter. I distanced myself from people who I felt were throwing negativity at me like confetti. This wasn't easy. In fact, I was in a state of shock, anxiety, and liberation for about a month. I remember being so nervous that everyone would leave me, even those I was being genuine with, because I wasn't acting like the person they once knew me as. I was so anxious that people were going to hate me even more than the fake version of myself. I thought for sure that no guy was ever going to come my way, and that I was going to eat my family out of house and home because of my emotions. But, I was wrong.

To my surprise, where one person exited, a new one entered. I came clean to those in my life who I felt I was being dishonest with, explained my newfound perspective, and to my surprise, I was embraced with love. Granted, some were not as kind, but it helped to support my decision to make room in my life for those who were going to lift me up. I started to feel better about myself. I started to feel less stressed, the negativity was dissipating by the day, and overall I was happier. I felt like a weight had finally been lifted off of my shoulders, and from there, the good kept coming. I was finally becoming heartbreak-proof.

Right around the time of the miraculous breakthrough with myself and my life, the COVID-19 pandemic came crashing in, grinding my social life to a halt. At first, I was angry. I felt like I was finally making gains in my life, and I wanted to be around positive people and share my positive spirit with all those willing to listen, but the damn virus had other plans. I was so ticked off, I was spewing hateful words and negativity at a germ that didn't give two hoots what my thoughts were or what I was feeling toward it. I felt like life couldn't be more unfair. That was until I chose to embrace this new perspective of life that I was dabbling with.

Don't get me wrong, being in that quarantine while living at home with my parents and having to teach from home was tough. There were many days when I would wake up and question if my life was actually happening, or if I was just in a deep, deep sleep. Unfortunately, I came to terms with the fact that it was indeed real life, and I had a choice to make. I could fall into my old habits of negativity and lies and stories, or I could take the time that I never had before to evolve into who I was meant to be.

I began meditating, researching, exercising, and eating healthy. I woke up with gratitude and spent less time on social media, and more time playing games with my parents. My brother ended up moving home, and I poured energy into making our relationship stronger. I stayed connected and strengthened my relationships with my friends that were lifers—shout-out to all of you reading this today!

The COVID time sucked ass, but in retrospect it was one of the best things that could have happened to me. Similar to the veil I was wearing while lying, my life was under this veil of constantly going and not resting. I was always on the chase of a new project, oftentimes bringing on new stress. I had little time to meditate, expand my mediumship business, explore new hobbies, or spend quality time with the ones who started the journey of life with me. The pandemic gave me the break I needed from life, and the chance to further my reflection on where I wanted my life to go. I was so young and had so much life ahead of me. I didn't know what I wanted to do or how I wanted to do it, but what a perfect time to find out! I started blaring my Morgan Wallen soundtrack on full blast in my basement apartment while searching high and low for all of the things that brought out my passions. And before I knew it, "Chasin' You" turned into "cashing in": becoming heartbreak-proof and living my dream life!

We all can relate to something similar to my story. We all wear veils of all kinds to mask who we are. Some of us come off cocky and confident to others to help mask our insecurities. Sometimes we remain shy around others in order to preserve our feelings from being hurt. We all wear a veil in order to protect ourselves from the world around us, but what good does that do? We all have a uniqueness to ourselves that was meant to be brought to light in this lifetime. We have qualities, stories, and perspectives that are meant to be shared and enjoyed with others. It's time we stop suppressing them in order to appease others and to avoid getting our hearts broken. For the majority of my childhood and early adult life, I couldn't fathom someone seeing the real me and possibly not liking me. It hurt too much, and the fear of being alone was too much to bear. But what cost does faking it 'til you make it have on our own self-love?

You can't love yourself if you refuse to let the world see you.

All those years ago, when a dear friend told me that I wouldn't find a boyfriend until I loved myself enough, I thought it simply meant amplifying the qualities I thought others would like. God, was I wrong. Loving yourself is being genuine. Find those qualities in yourself that you love and amplify them! Maybe you have a heart of gold that is constantly looking to give. Show that! Perhaps you have a strong sense of leadership that will help change this world. Take charge! Or quite possibly you have a sensitive side that allows you to empathize and sympathize with almost everyone. Do it. Whatever your pure qualities are, own them. They were given to you for a reason. You were given these qualities in order to have purpose in this world. Hone in on your awesomeness, and you will spend less time becoming heartbroken, and more time becoming heartbreak-proof and loving who you are.

Be kind to yourself. Love yourself for who you are. Don't put a mask over the parts of you you're scared others won't like. Share your opinion, be that leader, be kind and loving to the people that need it. I promise you by doing so, you're going to find your purpose in life and discover what this world has to offer you. The right people will become more attracted to your energy that you're putting out, and more opportunities in your life will become more aligned. If you have negative qualities, like my lying, change them. We all have them, and it's okay. Give yourself the love, patience, and acceptance that you're not perfect. Be humble enough to know that you have areas to work on. At the end of the day, we all do. To this day, I still find areas that I want to grow in and make better for myself. That's human! You're allowed to have flaws. What you're not allowed to do is create a version of yourself that isn't real. Please, please, please, don't wait as long as I did. Meditate, dig deep, and discover what's under all of the layers. Let the authentic you shine.

Think of it like real wood floors. In the '80s and '90s, it was "in" to put linoleum over them for a shinier appearance. Now that we have some sense in us, we're starting to realize that the real wood floors were more beautiful than anything you could have put over them. The same holds true for you.

I dare you to sit with yourself and reflect on those in your life. Choose one person and metaphorically sit with them. Think about how they make you feel, what happens when you typically hang around them. Now, give yourself love. Accept that person for who they are and how they make you feel. If you don't like it, change it. If you can't change it yet, find a way to create space between the two of you. Maybe just journal about your relationship with them. Whatever resonates with you, just let it go. Stop giving them the power to consume you and make you act disingenuous. See who you are, deeper than that. Who and what makes you feel good, or what do you absolutely love about yourself? There's hundreds of things, but just pick one. Once you hone in on it, think of ways to amplify it.

The purpose of the above dare is to get you in tune with who you are. As I have said and will continue saying, it is scary and hard. Nobody likes to dig deep in mud in order to reach the pot of gold, but the gold is worth it. So are you. Take the time to discover the real you underneath all of the b.s. and people who have consumed you for so many years. You deserve to live the most fulfilled life possible, filled with endless opportunities and limitless amounts of self-love. The way to do that? Start digging deep and find those qualities in yourself that are worth loving. And if they're not, work on them. I promise you the sooner you begin discovering who you are, the sooner your life will begin to open up for you. And of course, the sooner you will become heartbreak-proof!

CHAPTER 10

Unconditional Love with my Highest Self

Whoa baby. We have come far from the first chapter. You didn't think you would be finding yourself digging so deep within your own soul to find love, did ya? Jesus, you probably picked up this book thinking I was going to give you the secret that would lead you right to the fountain of love and becoming a cold-hearted a-hole, which would make you heartbreak-proof. You maybe thought by the end of this book (or near-end) that you would have seven dates lined up with the intention of breaking their hearts instead of your own. Little did you know that becoming heartbreak-proof comes with so much self-reflection, discovery, and connection with yourself in order to love. This chapter is one of the final "lesson" chapters, and in my opinion, one of the most fun.

You read the title right ... highest self. No, it's not the tallest version of yourself, so those of you who are 5'4" and under like myself are still in good shape! Your highest self is just another word for your truest self, the real you, the inside homie, your soul. Whatever you want to call it, it is the person you are when you remove yourself from your physical body (not actually, but ... you'll see). It's your ultimate existence and the qualities that you connect with the most in this world. Call it what you want, but I will continue calling it "your highest self" for this chapter. This part of self is the version of us that is brought into this world from the day our mamas give birth to us. It is who we are when we are the youngest, most vibrant beings of ourselves. Ever heard someone say that kids are full of life? That's because they are living their highest selves out. So what exactly happens to our highest selves? Well, young grasshopper, let me enlighten you.

Like I said above, when our mamas give birth to us, our highest selves are brought into the universe. We are born with a sense of who we are, the personality we have, and actually a sense of what we want in the world (crazy, right?). Over time, our ego begins to form. *Duh, duh, duhhh.* Just kidding, it's not all that bad. Our ego is our sense of consciousness that we develop from those around us. This includes family, teachers, neighbors, community members, and even society. Our ego is like our "protector" of our soul. The purpose of our ego is to keep us in check so we don't do things that will get us hurt, make us outcasts, go against the status quo—you name it. Our ego has good intentions, but over time, it begins to take over our bodies, mind, and spirit until we become our ego. The biggest difference between our ego and our highest self? Our ego is physical: what we portray to the world. Our highest self, on the other hand, is internal, and is what we aspire to obtain most in our world.

I can remember my junior year of high school being the moment when I finally understood that there were two different versions of ourselves. I was sitting in calculus class with one of the most logical and concrete-thinking teachers I had ever had in my life. I mean, this guy had "black or white" thinking, and very rarely strayed into the idea of intuition, let alone ego versus highest self. However, one day we started a conversation about future careers. My calc class included several seniors, many of whom did not know where they wanted their lives to take them the following year. I remember some of my classmates firing off ideas as to what they could study in college or what career would bring in the most money. At that time, I was currently struggling with where I wanted to look at colleges and even what I wanted to go for.

About three minutes into the conversation, Mr. S took over. I can remember sitting in the front row as clear as day, gearing up for him to tell my classmates to be logical, think about what will earn the most money, hone in on what jobs are open, blah, blah, blah. That is what every teacher and every adult in our lives were talking about. But instead, he took a different approach. He asked the kid what he wanted to be when he was five years old. Surprised, my classmate murmured something. Mr. S smiled at the answer that was given and responded, *"Then that's what you need to do."*

We were all beyond perplexed at this point, because we were pretty sure our stoic calc teacher told an eighteen-year-old high-school student that he needed to pursue a career that his five-year-old self wanted to pursue. Stunned, I looked between the two people until my teacher began speaking again.

"When I was five years old, I wanted to be an architect. I would build with my Legos, wooden blocks, sticks; anything I could find to build with, I did. I used to draw blueprints of buildings on old scrap paper and then build them, compare them to the drawings, and marvel at the talent I had. I would ask my parents or siblings what type of house or structure they wanted me to build them, I would sketch it, and I would build it. I could just do it. That was my biggest dream when I was younger, and I wanted to become that more than anything. As I got older, I heard how hard it was to make your own architect business from scratch. My dad would tell me I was unrealistic, and society told me I needed a more stable job. My teachers told me I needed to go to college.

"I went to college and was unsure of what I wanted to do. I did engineering for a while and hated it. Eventually I found a way to earn a teaching degree and worked at BOCES for a while building machines and enjoyed it. It was somewhat what I had always wanted to do. And eventually, I became a teacher for you guys. I taught you guys how to calculate hard problems and create science experiments or solve mysteries with the laws of the world. I was building the minds of the future. I like my job and I love my life, but part of me always wonders what I would have been like as an architect or how my life would have been different had I chosen that life despite what everyone else told me to do. So, when you start to think about what you want to do with the rest of your life, I urge you to follow the

dream you had for yourself when you were five. Kids know how to have a dream that can come true better than adults do. Think about it."

Hot-diggity-dog. The fact that I still remember the conversation as vividly as I do will always blow my mind, but it shows the significance of what this chapter is based upon: our highest selves. We're born with them, we hide them, but ultimately they are what we need in order to live our lives out of love and become heartbreak-proof. From the time we are children, our highest selves see the world with bright eyes and bushy tails. Nothing is out of reach, and everything we dream we can achieve. Hello manifesting! Over time, we get told by adults (who have already had their highest selves shut down for years) that we aren't capable of achieving certain dreams, we're being unrealistic, and we just can't do something because it's impossible. You get the picture. The more we are told these negative comments, the more we shut down our highest selves and engage more with our ego that is trying to help us assimilate to their world and people around us.

Ugh. What the fudge? Why does life have a way of taking a round out of us all the time? Did you find yourself playing into that line? That's your ego pitying yourself because of the way we have been taught to live. Instead, we are going to start retraining our egos to allow our highest selves to come through more often, so we stop becoming heartbroken over everything that happens in our lives. You got this! We got this! I won't leave ya hanging! Are you ready for your first step?

Repeat after me: I can do and be whatever I want to be! Scream it! Run around your house and say it over and over again. The more you say it aloud, the more you're fueling your highest self to come out! Because here's the thing—our highest selves never really go anywhere. Yes, it gets covered in layers and layers of ego, but ultimately your highest self never goes away. It's one of the biggest parts of who we are as people! And you want to know the absolute best part?

Who am I kidding, of course you do. Here's the secret you've been waiting for:

Once you unlock your highest self, you unlock
unconditional love and become heartbreak-proof!

That's right. You heard it here first, folks! Our highest selves have unconditional love for our physical selves, which ultimately help us to become heartbreak-proof. Hate the way you look in those shorts? That's your ego saying that your body doesn't fit the mold of societal beauty standards you've grown up with. Your highest self sees you strutting down the runway during New York fashion week with those babies! You crack a joke that no one notices or laughs at? Your ego is telling you that you're stupid for making that joke, and now everyone thinks you're weird. Your highest self is bent over, slapping their knee because they enjoyed the joke just as much as you did (which is why you said it!).

Think about it! A large part of who you are is your highest self. Our thoughts that run through our head, whether it be a great new way to get the company some money, an outfit you want to wear downtown, or a hobby you want to try, are the ways in which our highest selves are begging to come forth!

Ready for the craziest part? Since we are born with our highest selves and they really are the people we are meant to be, they never go anywhere. In fact, our highest selves sit inside of our physical bodies our entire lives until we're ready to let them run wild in order to obtain the lives we want, and give/get the love we deserve.

However, since our egos take over the majority of our decisions, thoughts, and actions, our highest selves begin to manifest in the form of desires or attraction. For example, you may find "your type" to be outgoing, adventurous, and beautiful beyond belief.

Dude, guess what? The reason that's "your type" is because your highest self wants to see a reflection of what you have on the inside in physical form. Because you refuse to let your highest self out, it begins to manifest in the form of attraction in other people. If it's not in a significant other, it can be in friends, strangers, TV stars, and role models. You name it! Our highest selves want you to find these qualities attractive in others, in hopes to allow yourself to let your ego down and your highest self shine!

Parallel to my self-discovery, I simultaneously found my highest self. The poor girl was found in, you guessed it, meditation. Personally I chose to name this version of myself "Hails," which is a nickname I had always wanted others to call me. However, upon discovering your highest self, you may feel more compelled to label them with your own name, or even a name that is completely different from yours! Either way, find a name that resonates with him/her, and begin stepping into that version of yourself!

Upon finding my highest self and sitting with her, I began to realize that many of my passions, talents, qualities, characteristics, and personality traits were within my highest self. When I would meditate and see this version of myself, it was as if I was looking into a mirror in a different dimension. The girl I saw looked an awful lot like me, but was different in some profound ways. For example, she had long blonde hair, whereas I had short brown hair. We had the same eyes, mouth, nose, and face shape, but she was about three inches taller than I was. She also was thinner. I felt oddly attached to this version of myself, and I found that I wanted to know more. I would ask her questions in meditation about who she was, what she was like, and what she wanted to do with her life. Before I knew it, she was answering those questions as I would have for myself.

I heard qualities and personality traits such as kind, funny, intelligent, caring, empathic, intuitive, confident, ambitious. She wanted to travel in her life, find meaningful relationships, teach, help and inspire others. She told me she was a part of me, just like I was a part of her. All I had to do was embody those characteristics myself in my everyday life. She told me to stop hiding and second-guessing, and start living. Although this made sense and resonated with me, I was still confused with how it all related to myself. I began feeling doubt and second-guessing my ability to portray this new version of myself. At that moment, she showed me a picture of myself that I remember fondly from when I was a kid. I was standing in our old living room with a scarf around my neck, a funky outfit of all sorts, laughing with the biggest smile on my face, a bucket hat and sunglasses. I looked like a hot mess, for lack of a better term. But, that picture was beyond special for me. That was the picture my parents had chosen for me to put in my senior yearbook. Below the picture they wrote, *Never lose your sense of humor or your ability to make others laugh.*

In that moment of flashing back to that picture and the quote in my yearbook, I found that the person I was on the inside was the person I had always envied in other people. For years, I admired certain traits in others that I wanted for myself. I had always been drawn to funny people, but I was funny from the time I could talk. I had always wanted to be surrounded by those who were athletic, but I was a natural athlete myself when I put my mind to it. I loved having conversations with those I found intelligent, but I never let myself share my own intelligent thoughts because I was too scared they wouldn't sound right. My whole life, I had been letting my ego hide my highest self out of protection, but instead I was shutting down every trait I already possessed, and I was trying to find them in other people. I was allowing my heart to get broken by others who possessed these qualities instead of allowing them to shine through myself to attract the right people.

For the longest time, I would portray a version of myself that was similar to what was on the inside, but to the extreme. I tried to be the best version of what I thought everyone else found attractive and what I found attractive in others, only for it to be thrown back into my face and ultimately break my heart. Every person I had ever come into contact with, I would try to impress by being overly funny, overly dramatic, overly calm, overly everything that was not the true me. I would convince myself that I was all of these labels that really weren't me. I would even form opinions and morals to live by because I thought that satisfied others, but it wasn't what I really felt. My ego was stepping in to protect me against society, to help me assimilate, but all it did was give a false side of my true identity and move me further away from loving myself unconditionally. It got so bad that one week in my senior year of college, I returned to my dorm after a campus-wide party (and me pretending to be the hyperactive, funny, pretty, calm, smart, flirty, overexperienced, sexy cheerleader I labeled myself to be) to cry for three hours in disgust of who I thought I was. I led myself down the road of heartbreak following my ego in order to find my highest self reflected in others who didn't give a rat's ass if they knew me or not. *So* not heartbreak-proof!

I can remember lying in bed questioning myself over and over and over again who I was. I couldn't think of a single value, thought, idea, personality trait, action or even dream that belonged to myself anymore. The lying, the portraying, and the straying from my true identity led me down a road of attracting people who only loved me under certain conditions. I found, time and time again, that when I broke out of my role of who I was pretending to be, these friends, partners, and strangers would become unattracted to me. I started to believe that I was unworthy of love, and I fell into the same spiral I had been in before of relying on external love to define who I was. I was a complete stranger to my own self, and that was when I decided to change. I started my adventure to self-discovery: who I really was. I wanted to know what really made me laugh, what felt natural to me, how I wanted to live my life, and what dreams I wanted to discover for myself.

This took days, weeks, months, and to be honest, a couple of years (cue the *Friends* theme song). I mean hey, I'm still trying to do this. I would meditate, trust my gut feelings and intuition of what felt right, and cut out the people I felt were weighing me down. One of the most important things I did was sit with my ego and ask myself what I wanted love to feel like. How did I want to bring in love? How did I want to feel when I felt "loved"? What did "love" look like to me? I asked several questions, journaled, and sought the help of my therapist, colleagues, friends, and family to help me find those answers. I spent many nights lying in bed, questioning myself to find the exact answers to these questions, and began searching my soul for how I could answer them. I wanted to become heart-break-proof to everyone who came into my life—meaning that I didn't feel empty anymore when those not intended to be in my life left.

I knew I wanted to feel attractive. As mentioned previously, I chose one of my first steps toward loving myself unconditionally as downloading Noom and starting my quest to lose weight.

After I began to feel more confident in my physical appearance, I decided it was time to tackle the mental side more. I wanted to feel honest, true, genuine. I wanted to love my thoughts, ideas, and emotions and feel like I could portray them around anyone. I chose to look into formal counseling, shared what was on my mind with my mom, and even used my voice to share opinions on the world or new innovative ideas with my friends. Once I started to put the ball into motion, it began to gain momentum.

I then wanted to tackle my spiritual state. I wanted to become elevated and open-minded. I wanted to find different avenues to explore possible career options. I wanted my physical space to reflect the love I was finding for myself. This included the people in my life, the job I was doing, and even the attitude I had on a daily basis. I started to look for any and all self-help books I could find to crack the code of love, specifically, attracting it into my life for the long term (ten out of ten would recommend *The Soulmate Secret: Manifest the Love of Your Life with the Law of Attraction* by Arielle Ford for some great tips and tricks!).

Once I started to discover my true self and the feeling of love that I wanted to feel for myself, I realized how simple the whole process was. I found myself questioning why I hadn't started being genuine with myself from an earlier age, and why more people weren't engaging in the same process. I realized all too quickly that my true purpose in life and the reason why I had to go through my journey the way I did (ya know, rock-bottom and all), was to help any and all people I could to find unconditional love for their true selves in order to become heartbreak-proof. That is what led you to me, with my book in your hands.

You chose this book for a reason. The cover, the blurb in the beginning, the first page—something stood out to you that made you want to learn more. I am here to start your ball rolling toward self-discovery. I am here to tell you that you are worth every ounce of love that you can pour into yourself. I want you to know that you deserve this journey just as much as me, your friends, or that random person on the subway. Self-discovery of your highest self is one of the greatest gifts we can give ourselves. It's a way of finding our souls in this crazy world we live in, aligning with them, and making this planet worth living on. Finding who you are and what you need helps you love yourself exactly for who you are.

Remember what you wanted to be when you were five? Go do it. You want someone to tell you you're attractive every day? Look in the mirror and do it for yourself. You want money to come flowing easily into your life? Begin telling yourself you're capable of doing whatever you set your mind to and make that dough! I promise, once you start your self-discovery journey, the unconditional love you will feel for yourself will coincide. You will no longer allow room for others in your life who will break your heart.

Are you ready for one of your last challenges? I think you are.

Do me a favor, and think back to your childhood and what you wanted to be when you got older. If you can't remember, sit in this present moment and think of your wildest dream of something you want to do with your life. Go ahead, don't be scared. Maybe you were like me when you were five and your biggest dream was to be, and I quote, "a teacher who changed the world" (thanks, Mom and Dad). Perhaps your goal was to be a rockstar, astronaut, chef, entrepreneur. Whatever it is, really let it come to mind.

Got it? Now think of what you would have to do to obtain that dream. Would you have to move? Would you have to save up a certain amount of dollars? Would you have to let the world know your hidden talents and put yourself out there? Whatever it is, make a list of those action steps you would need to take in order to get to your dream. Once you have your list, read it over, and share it with a loved one. Once we share our dreams with others, it makes them real. It shows the authentic souls that we hold inside because we don't want to sound silly (ego). Sharing it with someone also makes you more vulnerable, which helps you become heartbreak-proof!

This challenge is all about letting go of that ego, and letting the soul run free. It's okay to be scared of our dreams. But the reason we have the dreams we do is because our souls know what we are capable of. As I have always said: If you can dream it, you can do it! If you're really brave, start tomorrow on one of your action steps so you can start exploring your highest self, and the life that it entails. You'll run into a dozen other self-discoveries of your soul along the way, so just go for it. I promise once you do, that love will come right to you, sit itself in your lap, and give you that big ol' hug of "I love you" you've been looking for. Best of all? The more you follow your highest self and do what feels good for it, the more heartbreak-proof you'll become with every thought, dream, idea, and action you pursue!

CHAPTER 11
Dare to Dream

Imagine the song "Dream On" by Aerosmith playing on repeat as you read through this chapter. I promise you'll thank me later! :)

One of my biggest fears for the longest time was dreaming (aside from bugs, of course—if ykyk). I was scared of the dreams that I would have because that meant that I wasn't in the right part of my life. To me, when I would have dreams at night and wake up the next day vividly remembering them, I would think to myself, *Holy ghost, I am completely off the mark with where my life is currently.* I can recall waking up in the middle of the night with a cold sweat running down my face from a dream of me traveling the world. I was all over the planet, meeting new people, making others smile. I was teaching, meditating, learning, and growing. I looked angelic. In my dream I recognized the person I was looking at was me, but different on so many levels.

For starters, she had beautiful long hair that flowed like nobody's business. Her eyes were wide and bright and full of life. Her smile was natural, not forced. And best of all, she was fit, healthy, and what I deemed as thin. It was bizarre. I was so scared of that dream that I couldn't fall back to sleep. Now, I know what you're probably thinking—why the heck was I scared of a dream where my life looked pretty much perfect? Simple. I was scared that I was failing so much at my current life that my dream was mocking me for what I couldn't have.

My parents tell me I had the imagination of Dr. Seuss from the time I was little. I used to play with my dolls religiously and pretend they were my real sisters. We went on various adventures all over the world, getting into mischief and creating a bond that I wanted more than anything with friends. When I was little, I wanted nothing more than to have a sister. When my mom told me that wasn't happening, I decided the next best thing would be to have a friend that was like a sister. I went years searching for the perfect friend, but to my dismay, the girls my age wanted nothing to do with me. In fact, for most of my childhood my friends consisted of my brothers and their friends. My dream of having a sister, or close to one, was never coming true. I was failing at that dream.

As I got a little older and *Hannah Montana* was the new rage, I then had a dream of becoming a famous singer. Except, I didn't really want to become famous for singing. That was after I found out that my voice made ears bleed, but that was beside the point. No, instead I wanted to become famous in order to be a role model like Hannah Montana was for me. I spent days practicing my singing, taking videos of myself, and coming up with a catchy stage name. After watching each clip of me singing and realizing my own ears were bleeding, I threw down my notepad, chucked my recorder across the room, and sulked, realizing I was not going to fulfill my dream of becoming a famous role model.

Flash forward to my teen years, and my new dream was to have a boyfriend (Ha ha ha … please refer to all previous chapters). Ideally I wanted my boyfriend to end up being my high-school sweetheart, us falling madly in love with one another, traveling the world, having babies, and living happily ever after. To everyone's surprise, I was looking for a boyfriend in order to give my heart to someone in validation that I was enough. I wanted to know that I was lovable and that I was good, so finding a boyfriend who could validate that all for me was ideal. Guess what happened? That dream fell through the cracks, as I realized rather quickly that many boys at fourteen were not looking for a long-haul type of relationship. This is when my dreams really began to unravel, my self-love started going down the toilet, and my heart was breaking faster than you could say *Holy Hannah Montana* (I'm telling you, I was a superfan).

For years, I went through life without having dreams, or having other people make my dreams for me. Whenever I had the slightest dream come to myself, I would either ignore it or allow everyone else to give me their judgement prior to acting on it. Classic example—when I was a senior in high school, I had a dream of going to school at NYU to study education and get a minor in acting. I had always loved drama club (even though I refused to join because I was too concerned with everyone's thoughts about me), and I wanted to try it out in order to see if I would be any good. I wanted to move away from home, be on my own, and prove to myself and my parents that I could survive at seventeen at a college away from home. But, instead of acting on my dream, my parents told me I was just going to attend the community college in the fall where I would study education, because I was too young to move away. Don't get me wrong, they had my best interests at heart with what they said, but I never asserted my dream to them in fear they would never allow it. I was allowing my own heart to break.

I would be lying if I didn't tell you I had a lot of resentment toward them for pushing me in this direction. I was upset that they didn't care to ask where I wanted to go to school, nor did they try to look into schools that would be of interest to me. Beyond that, they didn't even hear me when I said I wanted to go to a four-year school instead of a community college to start off. It was already decided for me. No dream, no attempt, nothing. Lo and behold, I ended up attending said community college, hated it, and dropped out after one semester. My life was a hot mess for quite some time, and a lot of it contributed to the fact that instead of following my dreams and speaking up and choosing what I wanted to do, I let everyone else call the shots for me. All that came out of it was a period of miserableness, stagnant energy, missed opportunities and lots of heartbreak.

We all have dreams that we are dying to achieve. Unfortunately, we are brought up in a society where we are told that our dreams are just that: dreams. They are this unattainable thing that we think about at night as we're falling asleep, or when we're staring off into nothingness. They are glitz and glam, and more than likely a phase we are going through. After all, that's what I was told most of my upbringing. Don't get me wrong, my parents did support most of my dreams, but just like me, they were scared I was going to fail, so they didn't push me to attain my wildest, craziest dreams. You were probably brought up very similarly. Our parents are just as scared of our failure, to the point that they fail to realize the success that can come if we just pursue what our souls are calling us to do. Even with failure comes success, and a lesson that contributes to the rest of our lives of becoming heartbreak-proof!

Let me lay it down for you real quick. In short, dreams are brought to our attention because they are 100 percent achievable. From a spiritual standpoint, we are given our dreams because at some level we are aware that they are what we need to do with our lives. Our soul brings them forward to show us our capabilities, and to show us the life that we can potentially have if we just have enough courage to chase them. Now, from a practical standpoint, our dreams are not always achieved. More likely than not, they are not achieved because our fear of failure outweighs our hope of reaching them. In other scenarios, our dreams aren't achieved because on the road to achieving them, we stumble upon something else. A bigger dream, a greater outcome.

Dreams help to fuel our fire. They are our souls' way of showing us what our lives can be like. The dream I had all of those years ago that scared the pants off of me? That is my next greatest adventure. As I was traveling to Arizona for a long-awaited vacation, the dream dawned on me once more—I am meant to travel the world. I need to travel, meet new people, and eventually make a difference in the lives of kids around the world. I have always had a passion and dream to work with kids, mostly those with special needs, to help others see the potential and uniqueness they have in the form of an ability. I heard through meditation that my soul was calling me to go to Singapore to work with kids who have difficulty speaking. I would bring them assistive tech in order to help them get their voice heard. This was my new dream. I began working toward it, learning how to do this, pushing past my fears. I am hopeful to say, once COVID dies down and travel is allowed again, this will be one of my next destinations!

My dream of having a sister, or friends like sisters? That dream also came true. I stopped fearing the failure of friendships and instead started honing in on what I wanted in a friendship. I listened to myself, trusted who I was, and loved myself enough to put myself out there, and I became friends with people who are now like my sisters. They are of all ages, ethnicities, and proximities.

My dream of becoming famous was a bit off the mark, but I am a role model. I teach kids each day, and the amount of times I have been told by parents, colleagues, and students that I am their role model is humbling. I am making a difference in lives each day by following my dreams, being myself, and loving all of those around me.

My dream of becoming someone's sweetheart and giving them unconditional love? It has come true. I may not be dating someone I went to school with (or anyone at all), but I have hundreds of people in my life that receive my unconditional love on the daily, as well as reciprocate it back. I may not have kids of my own, but I have inherited several who I care for and have become a second mom to.

Dreams are in our lives for a reason. They paint the picture of how our lives can look if we are courageous enough to take action to make them reality. Dreams light up our soul, our world, and ourselves. What's your latest dream? What's stopping you from making it a reality?

I learned oh-so-quickly that once I release the fear that is holding me back, my dreams are exactly what I need in order to live the life I want. Our dreams come to us to show us the lives we have always envisioned. It's up to us to make those dreams a reality.

So what are you waiting for? Start putting your most recent

dream into your life! Keep humming the tune of "Dream On" and get after it! The more we act on our dreams, the more our hearts become heartbreak-proof.

CHAPTER 12
Calling Dave ...

As promised, I have an entire chapter of this book dedicated to one more story from my repertoire of relatable and embarrassing stories that ultimately led me to writing them down for you to become heartbreak-proof. The purpose of this chapter goes a little beyond just writing to resonate with you, but instead is a way for you to see that Daves all over the world are necessary. I do not have the words that appropriately thank Dave for what he gave me in this lifetime. Dave is part of my soul, and the true reason why I am where I am to this day.

Going into creating this chapter for the book, I was unsure if I even wanted to include it. After meditating and thinking on it for a couple of days, the reason why I needed to write this specific chapter came crashing into me like a ton of bricks—I needed to let go of Dave in order to accept the love for myself and make room for the love I deserve from someone else. Dave was the last straw that made me wake up and realize what I wasn't doing in order to become heartbreak-proof. If it wasn't for him, I wouldn't have had the realization I did in order to become heartbreak-proof.

You may have a Dave in your life right now, or maybe your Dave is waiting to come. Either way, you're beyond blessed. For this chapter, all you need to do is get in a comfy seat, maybe grab some tissues and popcorn, and get ready for this one. I promise, it'll tie so many things up and resonate with you in some aspect.

Sophomore year of high school, I was attending my new school with new friends, a new sports team, and a whole new sea of people who I had yet to meet. Pre-Will and even Jerry, there was someone who caught my eye from the second I started my new school. One afternoon as I was getting ready to go to field hockey practice, I had run into a group of guys that were in my brother's grade. One of them caught my attention, and he ended up introducing himself to me. He was kind, easygoing, and above all spoke to me on an energetic level. Dave walked into my life without warning, and absolutely had me wrapped around his finger without even knowing it. As I asked my friends about him, I was informed he was an ex-boyfriend of one of my teammates, and he was absolutely forbidden to date. With that in mind, I reminded myself to keep my distance, stay neutral with him, and above all, never EVER catch feelings for Dave.

We ended up becoming friends that year, exchanged numbers, and talked on occasion. I can specifically remember lying in bed one night texting him and thinking to myself, *This boy is going to change my life one day.* Oh, if I only knew then what I know now, maybe I wouldn't have waited so long for that change to come.

Junior year came around, and it was time to find a date for prom. As I had gained popularity being the "overly hyper, outspoken, cheerleading field hockey girl that was also Cori's little sister and Bailey's older sister," I quickly became friends with just about everyone in our small school, so I thought finding a date wouldn't be hard (can you say, *coincidence?*). The only problem was, I had an idea of who I wanted my date to be, and I would be darn sure that nobody stole him before I had the chance to ask.

As mentioned before, my sense of self during these days came from the falsity that I created for those around me. I came off as confident and that not much bothered me, but under it all I was a scared sixteen-year-old girl terrified of rejection and embarrassment. So, I went about asking the best way I knew how to. At an under-the-lights football game, I asked Dave AND about six of his closest friends who would be interested in going to prom with me that year. After flirting with five of them to get Dave's attention, his one friend (remember Jerry?) decided that he would jump at the bait and gave me a maybe. I thought that, despite my best efforts, Dave would have to wait for another day in order to be my prom date.

Well, that day did not arrive, because after inadvertently flirting with Jerry, the two of us began talking and then dating and, well, you know the rest because of chapter three. What you don't know is that throughout my entire relationship with Jerry, Dave was always in the background. He was always hanging out with us, inviting us over, and doing things here and there with us. We loved Dave. He was like a third wheel to our relationship, and I secretly loved every second.

Dave had an energy that was out of this world. He was upbeat, funny, kind, caring, intelligent, immature and mature all in one. He had the biggest heart for those he loved, and would give the shirt off of his back for anyone that needed it. To say I had a crush on Dave would be the understatement of eternity. I loved his soul existence. Whenever he was around me, I would become just me. This is not to say I didn't absolutely love Jerry with my whole heart, but the love I had for Dave was *different*. I didn't realize it at the time, but the reason why I was so attracted to Dave was because of the way he made me feel. Oh, the irony.

As years passed and I continued to date Jerry, I began to realize that I would find myself thinking about Dave. Dave eventually found a girlfriend, and I was happy for him, but it wasn't the happiness I had thought I would find. Instead I found myself feeling jealous, upset, and frustrated with myself. I began to pull away from Jerry without knowing it, and found myself daydreaming about being with Dave. Eventually I got so fed up, I went through a period of time refusing to see or think about Dave in order to push away the emotions I was feeling because of him.

Toward the end of my relationship with Jerry, Dave and I wound up at a party together. I was fighting with Jerry, Dave was fighting with his girlfriend, and we both ended up in the trunk of his car ripping shots of Grey Goose as we bitched about our significant others. Much was said that night between the two of us, but one thing I remember discussing was how much love we had for each other. We recognized each other's flaws, but at the end of it all we reassured one another what great people we were. I can remember to this day standing at the trunk not wanting the night to end, thinking about how all of this could be so different if I had just been myself four years ago and told him my feelings. Hindsight is 20/20, as they say. Dave ended our long convo by saying that Jerry was a good guy, and he was beyond lucky to have a girl like me. Woof, talk about a punch in the gut. After that night, I began to realize that Dave and I had missed our shot, and I needed to move on. It would never work between the two of us because he had so much love for both Jerry and me.

Eventually Jerry and I broke up over something silly, and my anger was not on him, but on Dave. I had heard a misconstrued version of a story that had happened one night at a rager, thought Dave had convinced Jerry to cheat on me, and decided that it was the perfect reason to hold a grudge against Dave. I chose to believe the story that I knew wholeheartedly wasn't true because I knew it was a way for me to validate my decision of moving on. And so, I started a new journey of finding someone else to fill the void in my heart.

Now, I'd be lying to you if I told you Dave was the only boy that pulled at my heartstrings. There were many other boys, Jerry included, that made my heart skip a beat. After Jerry and I broke up, there were several other obsessions I had with other boys, and eventually they consumed me to the point that I rarely ever thought about Dave. But Dave was something special, and I appreciated that for what it was.

About two years after my breakup with Jerry and my extraction of Dave from my life, I was out in Saratoga when I ran into Dave once more. Nothing spectacular happened. We said hello, took a picture, gave a hug, and on we went. To be honest, I didn't think twice about our encounter, but I can tell you I still remember the feeling I had after seeing him again for the first time in two years.

I was charged up, energized, excited, and stoked to have run into him once more. I smiled from ear to ear and felt a sense of calmness in my body. I felt normal, like I could let my guard down. I wasn't worried that he hated me or what everyone else around us thought about us hugging and saying hi. My friend who I was with that night told me I should try to go home with him because of how attractive he was, but I shrugged it off and pretended like I didn't notice. Because at the end of the day, it was never how Dave looked. No, that was never where my attraction grew from. Instead, it was the way I felt when I was around him.

After that encounter, I began running into Dave more and more. Each time we encountered one another, the people around us could pick up on the energy between the two of us. Many of my friends would comment on the way he looked at me, the vibe we put out for everyone else, and how I seemed so comfortable and happy when I was around him. To be completely honest, that was exactly how it felt when I was around him, too. After about two years of running into each other sporadically, we eventually hung out one night at a lovely bar in Saratoga once more. And this is where the ride really began. Buckle the fuck up.

After asking, begging, and downright telling me that I was going home with him, we made it back to Dave's apartment. We hung out, played cards, listened to music, and overall just relaxed. I hadn't been in an atmosphere where I could chill and enjoy myself with guys since the time I was young, but that is where I found myself that night. At about three a.m., I found myself preparing for what was about to come—a hookup with yet another person that I wouldn't talk to tomorrow. Despite my thoughts, I knew I had to sleep with Dave because it would be what he wanted, and it would give me a better chance of seeing him once more. Remember my lack of respect I had for myself? Here it was in action! Not to mention, it would be like living out a fantasy that I had had since sophomore year of high school. But, that's not how it happened. That's not even close to the way it had happened, actually.

Instead, we stayed up until five in the morning. We laid in his bed, talking and laughing. We caught up on what we had missed over the past couple of years, telling each other secrets, sharing stories that were intimate. It was like nothing I had ever experienced with another person before. And I never thought this would be the person or place I would experience something of this magnitude. The night eventually ended, and I still found myself preparing not to hear from him the next day. I slinked out of his apartment the following morning, but to my surprise, with him following closely behind me, kissing my cheek, and sending me on my way. Later that day? I even heard from the infamous Dave again.

The months passed, and Dave and I continued our "relationship." Eventually sex wove its way into it, but for a long while, we just enjoyed quality time with one another. It was as if we were friends again, like we had once been, but much more intimate. We only had eyes for each other, and everyone knew it. We had this way of understanding what each other was thinking without saying it, and there was an energy between us that we both knew was there, but we never spoke about it. I told him the darkest parts of my life that I had been through at that point, and he shared his with me. We would spend time with each other's friends and share memories and laughs until the sun turned into the moon and our eyes closed with happiness. The feelings I had were immeasurable for Dave. My heart was full. I was confident, vulnerable, and safe. I felt everything that I could have imagined feeling when you find the "love of your life." But, all good things eventually come to an end.

In October of that year, after the car accident and my grandmother's passing, I was what we youngsters call "ghosted." No more texts, phone calls, snapchats. No more randomly running into each other at the bar or making plans for dinner. Nothing. It was as if we had a messy breakup and he never wanted to see my face again because of how awful I was for him. Confusion, followed by anger, and finally guilt were just a few of the emotions that I felt when I was ghosted. I didn't understand why I wasn't hearing back.

At first, I thought I was too much for Dave. I thought he had finally had enough of the true Hali that he was given, so he walked away. Then I was devastated that I had actually opened up to someone, gave him everything that I had, and that wasn't enough. Finally, I felt guilty that I didn't do enough to keep him around. Did I not show him how much I felt for him? Should I have done more to make my feelings known? Maybe I should have toned it down or been more, maybe he would have stayed around? For three months (yes, I counted), I would wake up each morning and go to bed each night with a continuous record of thoughts coursing through my head of the "what ifs" or the "should have beens."

I know this sounds silly to some, but to me it was all I could do. I had to perseverate on the fact that Dave was gone. I had to know; I needed closure. This was my dream and my fantasy for so many years, and it finally came true. I told my friends and my family that I had the feeling I had found "the one" after all of this time. My friends and family adored Dave. I was myself, and let my guard down. I was fun while also being calm. I was outgoing but reserved. I waited to have sex. I only talked to and slept with him (with one exception). I had crossed my t's and dotted my i's, so what did I do that was so wrong for him not to want to stay around?

Looking back now on the situation, the hurt of it all still rings true. I loved Dave with everything I had, and I still care for him to this day. Yes, I was more of my true authentic self with him, and yes I had done everything "right" based on what society tells you to do in a relationship in order to get the guy of your dreams. But I was missing the biggest part of it all. I spent so much time thinking about Dave and what he wanted, needed, and desired. I helped him chase his dreams of his career, became what he needed me to be, hung out with his friends and did what they all wanted to do. Even though I was being my more authentic self, I was still loving him more than myself. And even worse, I was finding validation for love in him. I was hoping that I would feel loved by Dave and Dave only. Oh what a mess I found myself in.

Months had passed, and I hadn't figured out the algorithm yet. I was continuously plotting ways I could run into Dave so he saw how much I had evolved, how jealous he could be if he could just see me with another guy. That was until the day I finally ran into him at a bar in, you guessed it, Saratoga. We ended up getting into a screaming match in Gaff's, which resulted in the earth-shattering news I had known the entire time of the ghosting. For months, I was trying to fathom reasons why Dave couldn't love me based on who I was, but the entire time I knew that wasn't the truth. The truth was, as my intuition had it, Dave did love me. Dave loved me so damn much, it hurt his soul. The problem was that he loved me, but didn't love himself. He couldn't be selfish enough to love me and be with me when he knew ultimately he didn't love himself enough to be what I needed. He couldn't give up the habits I didn't love or his dreams that he was chasing to validate himself. He was scared to fix his past even if it made his future better. He wasn't ready. He was the exact mirror of who I was running from—myself.

His words hit me like a load of bricks, and they still reach my heart from time to time and pull on the strings. I would be lying if I said that night didn't completely and utterly shatter my existence. It wasn't a complete blindside, but it was enough to knock me off my pedestal of self-pity and into the phase of growth that had been begging to make its presence known in the past couple of months. In my more rational self, I knew that Dave was immature. I knew he had a scary past that he would need to grow from, but I also knew he needed to make that choice. I knew of his hobbies that he loved and the dedication he had to his career. I had known almost everything there was to know about the boy, and I knew deep down that the relationship was either going to be one where we grew together or grew apart. It boiled down to if we were both willing to work on loving ourselves while loving each other.

In the months that followed the original ghosting, I had known in my heart of hearts that I was giving up my life to dedicate myself to Dave. I stopped growing. I didn't care for my health, I wasn't worried about my career. I had almost stopped doing my mediumship business entirely, and I was a mega bitch to my family and friends because of it all. I began realizing with Dave's absence that my problem with attracting love had been in front of my face for so many years.

I am an all-or-nothing kind of gal. I will give my whole heart to anyone on this Earth, and leave nothing for myself. I will make up for the love that they lack for themselves with the love I have to offer them. I will give up my dreams, ambitions, goals, and drive in order to be their biggest cheerleader and number-one fan because I can always see the best of them when they can't see it in themselves. It took Dave giving me a chance that night in Gaff's to see it.

You owe yourself the love that you so freely give to other people. I found this quote while scrolling Pinterest one day, and it ultimately was a springboard for my growth movement within myself. I had found it post-Dave, post-ending it all on good terms, post-forcing the situation that was never going to work. I read that quote and felt it resonate inside of my soul. That is exactly what I have done since the time I was born. I have done this with my parents, my siblings, friends, acquaintances, strangers, enemies, boyfriends— you name it! I so freely give unconditional love to others. Although that is not a bad thing to do, it can be when you never give that same love to yourself. I felt like Pocahontas looking into the river at her own reflection that day I finally learned this vital lesson from Dave. I saw a boy who was scared to love himself because it meant doing hard things. It meant dealing with your past, getting out of your own way, stepping out of your comfort zone, and letting your emotions run wild. I was Dave in girl form. Instead of facing my problems and loving myself through them, I chose to focus my love on other people to make them better humans.

After twenty-three years of getting my heart broken, gaining weight, leading a life that I wasn't in love with, and most of all failing myself, I finally saw what I had been missing all along. I was missing the love I needed to give myself. I needed to fall in love with my life, my soul, and my dreams. I needed to stop fixating so much on being too much, not enough, authentic, beautiful, perfect. I needed to realign with my purpose in life and begin loving everything I had to offer this world. I needed to love myself so another Dave wouldn't break my heart again. I needed to become heartbreak-proof. I would have never had the courage to do that if it wasn't for Dave.

Dave was the second greatest love of my life. He is one person in this world who I will continue to have nothing but respect and love for, but he is not the one my journey will grow with. I know the greatest love of my life is out there waiting for me. Perhaps they're still learning this lesson for themselves. I realized after Dave breaking my heart that I needed to take the time to focus on me for once. No more excuses, no more investing in someone else's life. It was my turn to be my center of attention.

I deserved that much after all these years—and so do you. It is time to become heartbreak-proof. It is time to get our butts in gear and stop giving our love away like candy. That shizzle is valuable, and you deserve it!

Maybe you have a Dave story that helps you make sense of a horrible breakup. Maybe you don't, and perhaps this chapter has helped you reevaluate yourself and relationships. Are you someone who gives unconditional love to everyone but yourself? Ask yourself and answer that honestly. It's a scary thing to say "yes" to, for so many reasons. But, it's necessary.

Once we recognize that we're giving love out to others like its candy and we're the piñata we're left empty. We don't give ourselves love, and therefore we cannot attract it back from others in the way we deserve most. Maybe this chapter made sense to you, but you are married with three kids and don't know what to do. You don't love yourself but, you love your spouse and kids so much that you forgot how to love yourself. Dude, it's okay. You're not doomed. What you are is self-reflective and ready to start your journey to become heartbreak-proof.

Dave was an important stepping stone that I needed in order to begin my journey. I am thankful for him beyond words for the way that he treated me, loved me, and showed me my way. But as the saying goes, *I gotta go my own way.* No? Not a *High School Musical* fan? Well, whatever makes sense to you, say it aloud. Embrace this journey when you're ready. I promise you once you do, you'll never want to close the door, because you will become heartbreak-proof. Dave won't come into your life like a wrecking ball and destroy you like he did me without even knowing it.

You have to fill your cup with love before you start sharing it with everyone else. So, thank you Dave (not that you read this), but seriously, thank you. I wouldn't be me without you, and I definitely wouldn't have become heartbreak-proof if it weren't for us. I love you, and truly hope you're the millionaire-billionaire you have dared to dream you would become!

CHAPTER 13

Returning Home

As you can tell from the last chapter, Dave was the turning point from which I saw I needed to get myself together. If I didn't go through Dave, I would probably still be obsessing over every boy who was thrown my way in hopes that I could love them enough to get them to stay with me because my love was just that bloody good. After officially ending it all with Dave in the spring of 2020, I embarked on my most profound journey to date, which I like to call my return to home. It was wholesome, rejuvenating, and above all, kick-ass. It was at the point where Dave left my life for good that I found myself becoming 100 percent heartbreak-proof.

After graduating college in May of 2019, I legit moved home. And when I say I moved home, I mean I moved into our fifth-wheel camper that was sitting pretty in the front of our land as we built our new home (because remember, I burnt down the old one?). Picture this—my parents and I, living in a camper. How happy do you think my twenty-two-year-old self was at that time? Not to mention, I had some hot construction workers outside my window each morning pounding away as I grumpily laid on my folded-down kitchen table. Returning home was not joyful in the slightest bit.

I was bitter. Oh, was I bitter. I hated my parents for buying a camper for us to live in while our house was being built. I was bitter over the gorgeous construction workers waking me up every morning at 8:00 a.m. sharp with a saw. I was bitter over the sympathy and pity I was getting from others because I was living in a camper. I was so mad at myself for moving home, and above all, I was embarrassed. I felt like I had failed and I was a loser because I was living at home with my parents after completing my college education and starting my first real grown-up job in the fall. To say I was a failure in my own eyes was the understatement of the year.

Thankfully in October, a week before Granny died, I moved

139

into the new house. It was beautiful, shiny, and new. My basement apartment wasn't completed yet, but I had four walls and an actual bed to lay on, so I wasn't complaining. I finally had the feeling as if I was home for the first time in about a year, and to be completely honest, I was overwhelmed.

My first night in my new house, I began crying. I was upset with how bitter I was at my parents. I was grateful that the wait was over and I finally had a roof over my head that I hadn't had in almost a year. I was excited for new firsts in my new house. I was humbled that my parents were still willing to accept my grown ass to live with them. So many emotions washed over me in such a short amount of time. For the first time in a long time, I had returned home, and the amount of love I had was unparalleled.

My parents have by far been one of the greatest blessings I have been given in this lifetime. If it weren't for them, I wouldn't be the gal I am today. Not only did Big John and Tess welcome me back home with open arms after I graduated, they made life as amazing as possible. Dad was constantly cracking jokes and asking my opinion of how to make our new home so homey. Mom took on the role of my best friend and guiding angel when it came time to accommodate life back in my small town. They are heaven-sent angels that I am grateful for beyond words, and they are the biggest reason as to why I became heartbreak-proof to begin with. What did they do? They allowed me to return home.

Some of you reading this book may not have this option like I did. You may possibly come from the most tumultuous home in the world. To that, I say sorry, but home is not a place—it's a feeling. Home is where you can let your guard down and be yourself. It is the birthplace for our highest selves and where our unconditional love flourishes. This could be at a friend's house, community gathering, with neighbors, cousins, significant others, whatever. Your home is where you feel safest and most secure in being yourself, and where you are surrounded by others that make you feel this way. For me, I am fortunate enough to say my home is where I reside with my parents (or as I like to call them, my roommates). Returning home has always been and will always be my safe haven. When I'm with Tess on the patio, I know I can say anything on my mind and she will accept it without judgement. When I'm chillin' on the couch with Big John and need to get emotional for a hot second, I do so without a second thought because I know he will give me the biggest hug. We all need a place to call home in order to become heartbreak-proof.

After calling it quits with Dave, I was a mess. Like, full-blown mess. I would Facetime my best friends at night just to perseverate over the fact that Dave was gone, gone, and to that they would listen, empathize, and help me with kind words to move the eff on. After my house burned down and I was left with nothing more than the clothes I was wearing that day, my friends became my extended family and supplied me with more warmth and love than I even knew was possible. When my brother had gotten into his accident, my friends wrapped their arms around me in solidarity to let me know they were there to catch and support me. When Granny died, it was yet another time in my life when my friends came to the rescue in order to have a safe place to land after my head was done spinning around my body. My friends are another way that I have always returned home.

Although I now have the most amazing people in my life and I wouldn't trade their brutal honesty for anything, it hadn't always been that way. After all, I am a girl. I went through the girl drama in elementary and middle school, the nasty fights in high school, and the awkward assimilation phase in my early college years. I had more fallouts than successful friendships, but I am proud to say the ones who have stuck with me and joined me in recent years are my lifers. I can depend on them for anything (aside from keeping me sober when I go out in Toga), I can trust them with my life, and I love them unconditionally, as they do with me. They helped me to return home. They gave me the feeling of safety, love, and joy when I needed it most. They have helped me to love myself as they do, which in turn made me heartbreak-proof.

Along with my friends and parents, my brothers (as much as I'd love to give them no credit), are a huge reason I was able to love myself. You see, I'm the middle child of three, and I'm the only girl. My brothers treated me like a bro from the time I was an infant, and as a result I turned into the tomboy bullheaded girl I am today. My brothers have been my rocks for my entire life. They help to ground me in ways that nobody else can. They call me on my b.s. faster than anyone, and they are the first to come to my rescue when I become a hot-mess express.

Through my rock-bottom stage in my life and the months afterward, Cori and Bailey were my constants. Alongside me they stood through every tragedy, breakthrough, and revelation. Four years ago, when I told them I was a medium, I was expecting to hear what an absolute quack I was. But instead, they accepted me more than almost anyone else. They brought in business, asked questions, and gave me the support I needed to step out into society as who I was. In my lowest of lows, they're the shadows behind closed doors that are checking in on me, showing me love and appreciation. And of course, when I need to be knocked off a peg because I'm being a raging bitch, they are the first to call me on my dramatics and exaggerations. Needless to say, they have helped me to return home throughout my life. They have given me courage to embrace who I am at full force, while loving me in the most brotherly way possible. They have showed me through their actions and experiences how to become heartbreak-proof.

My point in this chapter is not to brag about all of those people I have in my life that help me to return home (although they are all pretty epic). I have a bigger point. Returning home isn't a choice or a privilege, it's a necessity. We all need people that help us to return home. I'm lucky enough to have shared a literal home with my people, but maybe you share a hobby or a career. Or maybe you share a passion or love with them. Whatever it is, hold onto those people for dear life. Grab them and love them and show them how much they mean to you. Because without them, without a strong base to help hold you up in your lowest of lows, it's that much harder to love yourself and become heartbreak-proof.

You may have twenty people you can think of right now that help you to return home. I hope you do. If you are the person reading this who can't think of a single one, know that it's okay. This does not mean you're doomed. I can remember a time in my life where I, too, felt like that. I felt like I was the one person in this entire world who didn't have a home to return to. I felt like an outcast, alone, and depressed. I didn't have people who made me feel safe or welcomed or accepted or loved. Trust me, I've been there. It was during these times I had to open my eyes wider and accept more than was right in front of me.

When I was fifteen years old, I was depressed. I hated my life more than anything in the world, and I felt like no one understood what I was going through. I didn't want to tell my parents what was going on, I didn't trust my brothers because I was scared they were going to tell my parents, and I had zero friends at the time. I had no sense of internal safety and love despite my incredible home life, and I hated myself because of it. I was burying my feelings with food on the daily, and I was crying myself to sleep in silence in order to somewhat cope with what was going on. I felt like the only person in the whole wide world who could connect with me at the time was Justin Bieber—trust me, I know his entire *My World* and *My World 2.0* albums by heart to this day.

I would listen to his music religiously, and would set up alerts on my iPod Touch so I knew when he was tweeting. Although I didn't know him personally, I felt okay and loved when I listened to his music. This was the first way I felt like I was returning home. I would listen to his songs at full blast, watch his interviews on You-

Tube, and even read books on him to feel like there was someone in this world that I connected to. As time went on and I felt a little bit better with myself, I began to express my emotions with Tess. This was the turning point where I realized there were literal people in my life who could be a safe place for me to land. They could help me love myself and return home.

So, if you feel like you have no one to return home to, know it's okay. You may feel like that now, but you won't feel that way forever. Pick a favorite artist, podcast, or movie star, and connect with them. Fall in love with their messages and the way they make you feel, and allow them to be the way you feel safe and loved and at home. Listen to what they have to say and embrace it with open arms. Check out groups of people who share a love for this person or hobby and connect with them. Those people may become your new home.

The point is, we all need someone to return home to. Someone who makes us feel loved for exactly who we are. We need these people in our corner, cheering us on, and allowing us to let our guard down. We need supporters that help to push us to the next level in our lives, and who challenge us when we need it. Returning home allows us to become heartbreak-proof, because it allows us to get in touch with our vulnerable side. As much as many of us don't like it (me included), we need to become vulnerable in order to allow others in. With vulnerability comes strength, and with strength comes love. Once you know yourself and are able to set the boundaries necessary to love yourself and return home, you become heartbreak-proof. You know who you want in your home because they make you feel good, and you know who to avoid because they make you feel like nothing.

It's a touch-and-go kind of game, and you're constantly working to return home throughout your life. With every person you meet, every new endeavor you explore, and every obstacle you overcome, you grow and meet new people who become part of your home. That's normal, that's part of life. We all have lifers, but we also all have those who can't hang forever. That's okay. It's not a bad thing, it's just life. The important takeaway is you have the lifers to return home to. Once you have them, you begin to love yourself more because they reflect all of the good within yourself. Once you love who you are, you become heartbreak-proof.

CHAPTER 14
Go Be Heartbreak-Proof

Well, well, well. Here we are at the most bittersweet part of every book—the ending. If you're anything like me, you anticipate the ending as finding that pot of gold you came looking for. It's the part where you find out that the boy got the girl, the widow found the love of her life from her youth (am I the only Nicholas Sparks fan here?), or you get that steadfast rule that you can start living your life from here on out. But this book has given you a lot to think about. I bet you picked up this book for a plethora of reasons. I bet you chose to read this book in hopes that this intuitive medium was able to offer a specific strategy or skill that you can walk away with and try for yourself. Unfortunately, that's not how self-love and becoming heartbreak-proof works.

You see, self-love is a process we go through in life. It is a journey. I am twenty-four years old, writing this book. By no means have I figured out the definite way to love yourself, or the one secret potion we can drink in order to cultivate being heartbreak-proof. What I can tell you is this: love isn't all around you. Love is something that you create within yourself. Love is the ability to look within your soul to see the connection you have with the Earth, and your divine self being on it. Becoming heartbreak-proof comes from you loving yourself enough to set boundaries, limits, and dreams for your life. You return home to your people after you've hit rock-bottom and you discover what lights up your soul. You are what your world spins around.

This book has been a manual to get you started on your final product. There were insights offered, but just because it worked for me doesn't mean that it's going to work for you. If that were the case, I would have stopped after I read *Girl, Wash Your Face* by Rachel Hollis when I was twenty-two and figured my crap out sooner rather than Daver ... later. Anywho, the point is, this is your journey. Your journey. Not your sister's, or your mom's, or your friends', or your coworkers'. Your self-love journey starts within yourself. Once you love yourself, you become heartbreak-proof. No one else has the power to hurt your heart again. It's that simple.

I wanted to wrap up this book with a few important points to make that I really, really, really need you to keep in mind later today, tomorrow, and weeks to come, long after you've read this book.

1. You have all of the love you want right inside of yourself. Remember, we envy qualities in others that we want to display in ourselves. And if we want those characteristics we see in other people, chances are they are innate within ourselves. Right now, start to embody those characteristics, qualities, and actions that you watch for in others. Go out in public and walk with your shoulders back, head held high, and a soft smile across your face. Wear that new outfit or flex your new lifestyle and be CONFIDENT. Own your physical look first, because we tend to get caught up in this one the most. Lose that weight, tone your thighs, dye your hair, or get that tattoo. Do what you need to do in order to take on what you feel is beautiful. No one else gets a say. Your significant other, family, and friends have absolutely no opinion in this matter because they don't get to determine your happiness—you do.

Once you have that physical presence down, start tackling the toughies. Start with the spiritual. What do you believe in? It can be anything under the sun. For me, it was spirit. It was knowing my angels and loved ones that had left this physical world were my guiding hands in this life, and I value them and their wisdom. I worship the higher powers that be, and allow them to take control of the situations that I cannot. I know their divine intuition and guidance will lead me down the path that I need to be on: one that aligns most with my soul. That is what makes me less anxious and less alone, and helps me to return home most days. I know that I have many looking over me, planning my life, and taking control so I don't have to worry about everything I chose to do. Everyone needs something like that.

You don't have to believe in spirit like I do, but perhaps you believe in God, Buddha, nature—you name it. Whatever it is that you believe in, connect with it. Practice the meditation to connect with it and ask your spirit to guide you. Put your trust in the fact that this universe is here to work with you, not against you. Feel safe, secure, and attached to your faith because it won't leave you, no matter what. Begin to internalize the feeling that you hold value in something that will withstand the greatest storms and incredible journey that you call your life.

When you're ready, tackle the mental. This was the hardest part for me, and I know it is for so many people who I have helped throughout my years of being an intuitive medium and teacher. Trust yourself and your higher guide enough to know that you are tougher than what you have endured in your life. If that wasn't true, you wouldn't be reading these words today. Your past doesn't define you, so stop letting it. We as humans get so "stuck" in past traumas, memories, and stories that were written for us that we become them. Stop it. Unwrite the story, turn the page, edit the memory, and forgive the trauma. You cannot fix it, you cannot change it, and you cannot run from it. By holding onto the past, we hold onto the emotions associated with it, which negatively impacts the way in which we live moving forward.

Make the conscious choice to move forward instead of staying still. You, darling, have spent too long moving back and staying still. It is your time to step into the light and deal with the anxieties that has been holding you down. Seek the professional help you need in order to heal your soul. Not one for counseling? Try meditating by yourself and bringing back some of the memories that haunt you. Start by first replaying the memory, and exposing yourself to the emotions you felt when it happened. Now try thinking of that same memory with a different ending—the ending you wish there was. After you've done both, accept that although the ideal ending didn't happen, you have the courage and knowledge to not make the same mistake twice in order to relive the past, and believe that. Surround yourself with pink light and love, and tell yourself it is okay to feel what you have felt.

Maybe that is too scary altogether. If so, then write. Write a letter or journal your feelings. Go for a run and think through what it is that is hurting you so much that you just can't love who you are. No matter what your outlet is, you need to work through the memories and emotions that are holding your soul hostage and preventing you from moving forward. It will suck in the moment, but I promise after five minutes, you will feel relief. You have control over the situation now, and you know that you have already beat it. Relief and healing will follow once you give yourself the chance to work through it. You are stronger than you think!

Tackle these three parts of yourself: the physical, spiritual, and mental. It's hard work. This is the hardest thing you will ever do, but I promise you it will make you become heartbreak-proof. For me, once I began working through some of the mental blocks, I felt a sense of love blossom within me. I began having more gratitude and a new sense of beauty that I had never had before. After I tackled the mental, I felt strong enough to push harder on the physical. I began working out more, changing my eating habits completely, and encouraging my family to do the same. I challenged myself every day with more "hard" things, and the results showed it was worth it. Whatever feels best for you, do it.

You have all of the love you need right inside of you. It just may be hidden under your insecurities, subconscious, or past. I promise, you have all of the power you need to unleash your self-love, and to become heartbreak-proof, you just have to want it bad enough. And trust me, you do, because you've made it this far. Stop envying the person you see walking by you with the perky pony and killer body—become them. Stop being jealous of Karen who sleeps for eight-plus hours a night while also being the PTO president and bake-sale queen—join her. Quit complaining that Richard in sales is getting promoted more than you—have him guide you. Once you get out of your own way, you become those that you envy around you. Just do it. Look in the mirror and love what you see; only this will make you heartbreak-proof.

2. Put yourself first. This right here; this is the golden rule of becoming heartbreak-proof. This rule is like telling the truth—they go hand in hand. If you are choosing to embark on this journey (who wants to continue getting their heart broken?), then you have to play by this rule. Believe it or not, this is one of the hardest tasks for my clients and myself to tackle. I mean, what does "put yourself first" even mean? Well, young grasshopper, how about I enlighten you!

Basically, it means: be selfish. It means do what the heck you want to do. Stop worrying about everyone else and their needs and their wants. What do you want? What is it that you've been putting off for days, weeks, months, or even years? There is always something, so don't try to back out of this one so easily. We all have *something* that we push off until tomorrow because it's just not convenient at the time. So what is yours?

Mine was a lot of things. Travel was one of the biggest. When I was growing up, my family and I always went on vacations, but many times they cocooned my brother's baseball tournaments. By no means do I want to come off as an ungrateful brat about any of the amazing places we traveled, because they were the most enthusiastic, blood-pumping, family-bonding-to-the-max experiences I could have ever had. Growing up, I recognized how fortunate I was to have a family that was able to bring us on a summer trip, not to mention I loved staring at baseball butts from the time I was five!

But as I got older and my family members developed lives outside of our home, I decided I wanted to continue the lifestyle of traveling. However, I was bored of the typical Florida, Maryland, Virginia trips. So, when I was a freshman in college, I decided that traveling was top on my bucket list of activities to do. I wrote down all of the places I wanted to travel, the things I wanted to see, and a timeline of when I wanted them to happen. I wrote down that by the time I was a senior in college, I would have already been to London, Barcelona, and Sicily. Well, here I am writing this chapter to you, and I can assure you I never have been to any of those locations.

You see, each time I was getting ready to look into a trip or even book one, I always found a reason that told me I couldn't go. At first, it was that I didn't have enough money. When I finally had enough money saved up, I didn't have a passport. Once I figured out how much a passport cost and where I could easily get one, I decided I had no friends to go with. Then there were increased terrorist attacks. Then my grandma got sick. Then I started grad school. Then flights were too expensive. Then I couldn't leave my family during such a hard time in our lives. Then COVID. The list went on, and on, and on to the point that I chose to just forget my plans of traveling, and to settle for the fact that I won't ever travel to Europe. I was a ball of excuses, and with each excuse I fed myself, I broke my heart just a little harder.

I would hop onto Instagram and get annoyed when I saw girls I went to college with enjoying their baguettes in Paris while I was sitting in my parents' house in upstate New York. I would get annoyed and frustrated each time I would plan a trip and my friends said they didn't have enough money or they didn't want to go. I would get frustrated with the fact that I was too scared to travel abroad based on what everyone had told me. I found myself constantly running into obstacles.

The same situation holds true when it came to my friendships for the longest time. Each time I found a friend, I found myself more concerned with if they were having a good time, if they were loved by me, or if they were happy rather than myself. I did the same with romantic relationships, and work relationships. Basically everywhere in my life where something or someone could come first, I allowed it to happen. I would constantly let other people do my thinking for me, make my decisions, and dictate what I was going to do. That's what happened in my relationships, and that's ultimately what happened with my dream of traveling.

After a while of feeling sorry for myself and wondering when my luck would change or the right opportunity would come around for me to actually travel abroad, I decided I needed to make a change. I was sick of living vicariously through everyone else. I was done wishing and wanting and falling short of following my dreams. I didn't want to hear everyone else's thoughts and opinions on what I should do or need to do because they knew better than I did. As I said right around the epiphany of my twenties, fuck that.

And that's exactly what I did. Around the time COVID happened, I had been talking with Gab about traveling and telling her how I can never find people who are serious about going places with me. We agreed that we have always had the dream and desire to travel to extraordinary places, but we were always putting other things and people first, so we rarely had the opportunity to do what we wanted. That night, we booked our trip to Sedona, Arizona, and never looked back. To say that was, and still is the most magical trip I've ever been on is the understatement of the year. And that was just the start of it all.

I began looking seriously into different places I could travel and visit that were on my bucket list. I stopped listening to other people and their opinions (especially the news), and I started to form my own opinions. I stopped perseverating on my friends' thoughts and feelings and I started to focus on my own. I became selfish in the best way possible. I started to mend my broken heart by putting myself and my dreams first for the first time in my entire life. And let me tell you, it worked.

If you're anything like me, this idea alone sounds nearly impossible. I have always had a bit of a bleeding heart, and will always be one who puts others' needs before my own. But at some point in your life (mine was at twenty-three), you get sick of that, and you begin to say, "Screw this." You get tired of putting other people first. Your energy becomes drained, you become distant from yourself and your dreams, and you may even feel depressed or empty. This is what happens to so many of us when we continuously put other people in front of ourselves. When we constantly go that extra mile to put the smile on someone's face who doesn't care to put one back on ours, or do countless favors for those who refuse to return it, or even build others up who wouldn't dare throw a compliment to us, we are depleting ourselves of the love we deserve. Those are the people and things we need to cut off. At least for a little while.

When we begin to put ourselves first, we are going to rock the worlds of a lot of people. This happened to me. When I began traveling, I started to aggravate people because I was using my money on plane tickets and experiences rather than food and booze. When I started to hang out with people who made me feel good about who I was, I angered the people who would take my energy free of charge without replacement. When I stopped agreeing out of ease and avoidance of confrontation and instead asserted my own ideas and opinions in a respectful manner, I had some turn their nose up to me and tell me I was living in an unrealistic world of peace. Face it, when we start attuning more with ourselves and putting ourselves first, we are going to drive people mad. It's because we are changing, shining our lights, and relying on ourselves for our love. We all want to be needed and wanted by someone, but we first have to need and want ourselves in order to do the same for others.

By putting ourselves first, we are choosing to love every aspect of ourselves fully before letting other people and things take over that control. Remember way in the beginning when we talked about what self-love was? Remember our talk a couple chapters ago about dreams? Both categories are fair game to pick from when we're talking about choosing ourselves. Do what is calling your name! Wake up and go watch that sunrise. Take that new course. Buy a new wardrobe. Take a break from social media for a week. Do whatever your soul is calling for you to do without even thinking about asking another person's permission. Choose you above others for a day, a week, maybe a month. Once you get the hang of it, continue choosing yourself until you can fall completely in love with every ounce that you have to offer this world. You are worth that. Choose you, and choose to become heartbreak-proof.

3. **You attract what you put out into the universe.** I know we've been over this one, but I felt the need to end the book on this final rule. If you put down this book in five minutes and never refer to it again, I hope this is the line that you carry with you on your lips for the remainder of time. I pray these are the words of wisdom you share with your daughter someday and your best friend over coffee. I wish these are the words that you remember when the world feels as though it is crashing down around you, and you feel nothing but hopeless.

You attract what you put out into the universe. This comes in the form of friends, relationships, mentality, job opportunities, experience, love. Everything. You are the creator of your own reality. I like to think of it as if we are in a video game. We are the player, the only player of our game. We are the ones holding the joystick or controller, and we're the ones pressing our buttons in order to make our character jump, run, cry; whatever. It's us. We hold the power over ourselves. As soon as you give that divine power away is the day the game is over. So keep that to yourself.

When you pick up a book such as this one, you probably think to yourself that this is going to be the secret ingredient you have been searching for your whole life in order to find your Prince

Charming or the ticket down the wedding aisle. Well, I'm sorry to break it to ya—but this isn't that book. Let's face it, you knew that deep down inside of you that this wasn't the book that was going to hold that sweet secret that you've been searching so hard to find. This book may not contain that secret, but the person holding it does. You. You have the power to bring in that love that you have been tirelessly looking for for days, weeks, months, or even years (cue *Friends* theme song once more). You hold the power of yourself, which evidently makes you heartbreak-proof to others.

For the longest time when I was growing up, I always thought that love was an external force that was brought upon by strikingly good looks and luck. I didn't know what it meant to love oneself, and I was definitely confused all those years ago when my dear best friend unveiled to me that I cannot be loved until I love myself. I didn't know what that meant, but now I do. I finally understand the secret to love, and the road that we all need to take in order to get it. I finally know how to feel heartbreak-proof. It's been so easy, right in front of me, and overlooked for so stinkin' long that it was almost unrecognizable. All you have to do is fall in love with who you are.

That simple. That easy. Start choosing you. Start finding the quirks about yourself that you love. Begin looking in that mirror and tell yourself how you're rocking those jeans. Make yourself laugh at the silly things that you do, and actually appreciate how silly they really are. Force yourself to feel your emotions. Cry when you feel like you have to, or dance when you're super excited. Fall in love with your passions, dreams, and desires and dare to chase them. Ask yourself what it is that lights you up, and go after it. Enjoy the journey that it takes you on. It may not have the desired outcome, but the outcome will be desired regardless.

Take your chances. Shoot your shot with your boss and ask for that raise or share your latest idea. Instill confidence in yourself. Meditate and follow your intuition on what you need most in your life in the moment that you need it. Trust yourself above others. Stop judging yourself—I promise you are your hardest critic. I know I sure was.

A month before I started writing this book, I was beyond lost. I was devastated without Dave, I refused to meditate, I hated working from home, and I was beyond depressed when I looked in the mirror. I was at my rock-bottom. I was spewing negativity, talking terribly about myself and others, and looking outside of myself for the love that I knew I desperately sought. I would be on dating sites swiping ferociously. I would go out with the intention of someone thinking I was cute enough to take home. I set the intention each time I hung out with guys that one of them had to look my way or else I didn't think I was good enough. I was doing the exact opposite of what I needed to do to attract the love I wanted so badly.

Meditation brought forth the idea of writing this book. I set out with the intention that I would look into the idea of writing a book based on the ideas I learned about in regard to self-love and becoming heartbreak-proof. I decided that I was just simply going to journal, then my journaling turned into ideas, and finally I stumbled upon the phrase "you attract what you put out into the universe." I believe I saw it on Pinterest, or possibly Instagram, but it resonated with me. I saw the phrase and understood that I needed to help others love themselves. I needed to get the word out that love isn't manifested in others, but instead in ourselves. When you give yourself love, the universe sees and delivers you love that matches the frequency you put out. Once you instill the feeling of comfort and vulnerability within your soul, you outwardly become heartbreak-proof to others.

In simple terms, the more you love yourself, the more the universe will see you cannot be broken by others. You will draw people into your light who love you equally. It may not come in the form of a relationship like you hope, but it will come in the form of mentors, kids, friends, parents, extended family, strangers, and coworkers. And the best part? The more love you attract and manifest in yourself, the more love that is put out into the universe. As a result, you begin to love your life even more. Those who are not meant to be in your life stay away, and those willing to accept and love you unconditionally for who you are come flocking.

So I suppose if you were looking for that secret this whole time, this was it. You have the power to attract that boyfriend or girlfriend or that amazing friendship. You have the ability to find the love that you've always dreamt of, but you have to have it within yourself first. The universe has a funny way of working with you to become heartbreak-proof. I have found religiously that no matter what I do, the universe is always matching my energy in the form that I give it. Over the past year, as I moved on from Dave and separated the idea of love from him, I found that when I give love to myself—that is, allow myself to express my emotions, travel, and invest my time and money in my own passions, I was attracting the same love from the world around me. I was finding friends who had similar interests and who were uplifting. I found myself becoming parts of groups where the positive messages I was telling myself were similar to that of others. I was loving waking up early to watch the sunrise, as were the beautiful creatures that were there to join me.

I guess I started this book looking to find the answer to my own question—how can I become heartbreak-proof, and how can I fly toward that destination fast enough to find someone at the end? But the answer was in front of me the whole time. I don't need someone else to do the loving for me or to show me how to be heartbreak-proof. I need myself to show up every day in order to love every inch of who I am. Once I can do that, I will find someone who complements that need for me. Until then, I will meet hundreds of individuals who share that same feeling. You can answer your own question that you had when you started reading this, too. What will lead you to becoming heartbreak-proof? Well dude, you're already there.

Put the book down and start loving who you see when you look in the mirror. Find yourself in this world, and be unapologetically you. Dance like nobody's watching, travel the world and eat all of the amazing food each place has to offer. Be bold and take risks. Follow your passions and live out your dreams. Whatever you do, do it for yourself, and love yourself as you do it. I promise once you start doing it, the universe will deliver the love you're seeking at your doorstep when you least expect it.

So there you have it. I guess that's the secret to becoming heartbreak-proof. Cheers!

Acknowledgments

First and foremost, I must thank my editors—Valerie and Ashley. From countless emails and calls, to giving me the ability to make my dream a reality, thank-you does not seem to do justice to what you two have given me. I appreciate all your hard work, your dedication, and your willingness to help a first-time author like myself. Likewise, a huge thank-you to Meghan for designing my beautiful cover. You helped take a vision and created a masterpiece from it. To Reilly, thank you for capturing the beautiful photo for the cover. My heart and love is sent to you all for taking my dreams and ideas, and turning them into a physical piece for others to enjoy.

To Mom and Dad (Tess and John), for teaching me that being uniquely me is OKAY. From the time I was little, you have both accepted me for who I am, and have encouraged me to never lose my sense of humor and dreamer lifestyle. You both raised me in a world where I had endless possibilities to become whoever and whatever I wanted. I certainly would not have written this book if it were not for you both continuously showing me unconditional love and support my entire life. Words and lessons you both have taught me over the years are undeniably traced in the pages of this book. I love you.

To Cori and Bailey, for being the two biggest pains in my ass I have ever had the pleasure of loving. Had it not been for you two, calling me on my shit, showing me new ways to live, and ultimately pushing me beyond my limits, I would not be sitting here writing my acknowledgement to you both. You two have given me the ability to look at life from a different perspective. You have taught me how to laugh at myself, but to stand strong in the face of others when it comes to pursuing my passions.

I love you both, and promise this book will only embarrass you slightly.

To my past boyfriends and flings mentioned throughout (especially Dave), for giving me the stories that needed to be shared with others. Each and every one of you who was woven into these chapters has given me the opportunity to grow into who I needed to become. Through the tears, smiles, and memories, I have been able to transform into my authentic self. You are all to be thanked, and I wish you all the best. If this book finds its way into your hands, know the immense amount of gratitude and love that I am sending you.

To Gab, Jord, Grace, Lina, Rebecky, Min, Georgie and others, for putting up with my crazy and inspiring me to achieve my dreams. You all have opened my heart in one way or another. Each of you have taught me lessons that brought me to the point in my life where I could love myself and become heartbreak-proof. I am grateful for the endless conversations, the car rides, the wine, the laughs that brought tears to my eyes, the ideas, and the support. I would not be Hails without my army of girls behind me. I love you all endlessly.

To my coworkers, for helping me juggle my big-girl job while also reaching for the stars. You people are beyond inspirational, and if it weren't for your constant support with lessons, kids, and life, I wouldn't have had the time to turn this book into a reality. Thank you for your smiles, hugs, and helping hands. You ladies rock!

To my kiddos, for showing me what it means to live life to the fullest. Every day I get to wake up and teach the most inspirational kids, but in reality, you are all teaching me. I am beyond thankful to have had the opportunity to be your teacher for the past three years. With every hug, conversation, and obstacle to overcome, each of you have taught me the true meaning of resilience and higher love. You guys have helped turn my life into something worth living, and I hope you get to enjoy this book with the understanding that each of you was a catalyst for it. Rock on, guys!

To my family and friends, for being a part of this journey throughout my life. I cannot begin to list each of you who have touched my soul in one way or another. Each interaction, conversation, and word of encouragement over the past twenty-four years have led me to this exact spot. You know who you are, and I thank you from the bottom of my heart for all of the love.

Hali Winch, commonly known as Hails, is a first-time self-published author from a small town in Upstate New York. Hails writes from the heart, exposing the truest and rawest forms of herself in hopes to create meaningful connections with and among her audiences.

From the remarkable stories of her past to her secrets engraved on the pages, her first book encompasses her triumphs and defeats that led her to the road of self-discovery and unconditional love.

A special education teacher by day, intuitive spiritual coach by night, and just a regular twenty-four-year-old girl on the daily, Hails lives a life led by love and passion. She can often be found looking for inspiration in others, while simultaneously inspiring others to live a life they dream of finding. Hails' stories encapsulate bad romance, body image and rock-bottom moments, but are targeted to enlighten and entertain others. Join her on the path of falling in love with yourself, as Hali describes the worlds we are able to create from within.

Looking to catch up with Hails?
Be sure to check out her website www.hailswinch.com.

Xo,

Hali Winch

Made in the USA
Columbia, SC
03 May 2021

37166657R00098